The Right Way

The Ultimate Guide For Aspiring Internet Entrepreneurs

Al Mubeen

Acknowledgement

Writing a book is not only an individual project, but it is also the teamwork. I thank my friends and family members who have been helpful during this process. Also, I sincerely thank people who gave me space to explore my passion and do what I love.

Contents

Contents

Contents

THE INNER LAYER
CHAPTER – 7

CHAPTER – 8

Contents

Preface

Are you currently stuck? Have you launched your beautifully designed online store, but don't know what to do next? Have you loaded the pet products, accessories, gadgets, and T-shirts, but nothing started moving out of the shelves? The Facebook ads are not performing as you think? You feel so embarrassed and stuck now? If you don't know what to do to get your first online sale, don't worry about it anymore! You are in the right place because I felt the same thing when I started my first online store a few years ago. The bitter experience I faced during that phase triggered me to write this book. It will be helpful for entrepreneurs to make their online business a profitable one.

In today's internet era, starting an online business is very easy compared to brick & mortar stores. The important thing is, you could set up an online store within a few hours, but many people are starting online business without knowing much about the factors that need to be taken care of before getting started.

When I started my first online store, I never bothered to know about the business prerequisites that should be known to start the online business. I watched a few YouTube videos that taught how to make 10k per month, and you could guess what happened next. Yes, I started my first online store within a few days. At that time, I don't know it will be a failure. I was interested in online business, but I don't know how to find the products that sell. I was in my MBA final year studies and started to research the online business and marketing strategies to kick start my next business, but that time I took it seriously because achieving overnight success is a myth. There is no shortcut to success, but anyone can be successful if we put correct efforts and hard work because there is no shortage of success too.

To achieve success in online business, you need passion, patience, focus, persistence, and lots of grinding. You can't just set up a store with some products and sell them to the customers with Facebook ads. I will tell you that this approach is a deceiving one. You want to know why? You will know that soon. If you approach business as I mentioned above no one will come to do business with you, and it will lead to failure and shutting down the store. That's what happened to me, and without a doubt, this is going to happen to you tomorrow if you do not take the right step.

I am not demotivating anyone here. I just want you to know the hard-hitting facts because ninety percent of customers don't buy from unknown websites on the first encounter. You know what? It is not rocket science because they don't trust you. Some studies also refer that 80% of online stores close the door within 120 days due to no sale. No wonder I did the same thing for my first online business.

Failure is not a bad thing. But being there for a long time without learning anything from it is bad. Many successful entrepreneurs like Danlok, Bill Gates, Mark Zuckerberg, and my favorite Grant Cardone failed in their first attempt. The current state never defines our future

state. The action is the only difference between successful and unsuccessful people. Taking enormous action is
the first step to succeed in any business. But here is the
catch, you need to identify The Right Way. If not, you
end up taking actions in The Wrong Way. Have you ever
watched E-commerce 101 on YouTube? They will teach
how to make money in the short term and achieve financial freedom. If you start a business by thinking that only
products and Facebook ads are enough to make money,
you will fail even if you take massive action. Take your
business seriously and work with passion because business success is not short term. The entrepreneurs should
work hard to scale the business.

The Right Way Thinking

In this book, you are going to take on the business journey in The Right Way. It is the core principle behind all
successful people in the world. Take any successful person in any field. They all follow The Right Way to achieve
success. You can ask me, what is it all about? I would like
to start with this line. "All things are created twice," says
Stephen R. Covey. There are a first creation and second
creation to all things. Likewise, the success also has two
creations one is the outer layer and another one is the
inner layer. Indeed, the outer layer is all about skill and
knowledge, and the inner layer is about you. These two
layers are needed to get high results in business. It's like
having the best car (Outer Layer) and the best driver
(Inner Layer) to ride it. If anyone of these caused trouble,
you can't reach the finish line. Because both are necessary
to reach where you want.

The business skill and knowledge are like a vehicle,
and you're the driver of that vehicle. If anyone of them is
not well, your travel will lead to failure. You will go far
only based on these two factors in business. And many

internet entrepreneurs will fall in any one of these two below. The first one is Half Way. In The Half Way principle, people will concentrate only on the outer layer. They will care only about learning business skills like marketing, finance, or knowledge of the business they want to start. But they won't care about the inner layer (that is nothing but themselves) or sometimes they would know both the layers partially. The Wrong Way is people who don't bother about the outer layer (that is the skill or knowledge) and also the inner layers (that is none other than themselves). If that is the case, those people will fail in everything for sure.

The Right Way principle is the correct one. And people who want to succeed in business should take care of both inner and outer layers. In business, people should get the necessary skills and knowledge. Also, they need to tackle procrastination, control themselves to avoid instant gratification. The barrier to you becoming successful in business is no one but you. One thing is very evident here. Because all successful people take care of both the outer and inner layers to achieve what they want in business. If they can do it, why don't you? That is what we are going to see briefly in the coming ten chapters. But I would like to remind you now that this book's principle applies not only to online business but also to offline businesses.

Having said that, this book has three parts (The Outer Layer, The Inner Layer, The Model). The first six chapters talk about the outer layers. You will know the critical skills that need to be learned to start an online company. And chapters seven, eight, nine talks about the inner layers. As I said, that's just "you." You will learn how to achieve your goals by preventing procrastination and instant gratification. And the last chapter is about getting started with The Right Way. There we will see some examples of both outer and inner layers. I am very much excited to take you along with me to go through this journey.

THE OUTER LAYER

CHAPTER – 1

"It is not about selling. It is about creating value for the target audience" – Jerry Allocca

What Business Is All About?

We usually think business is all about selling something to someone for a profit. Because most people care only about sales when it comes to business. But business is not only about sales. It is also about providing value for the customers and building a strong relationship with them. It is an exchange of values between you and customers for profitability. As an internet entrepreneur, you need to create more value through your business to customers in the marketplace. Always try to provide more value for the customers if want to be successful. I will recommend you to provide ten times more value with the help of your product or service than the competitors. It's possible only if you understand the target customers.

How to Get Started

If you're talking about starting a business online, or you might have already started it, and doing all things on your own. I understand because it's a common problem for start-up companies today. I call this a setting phase because you are the one who looks at the marketing, sales, operations, and finance. I forgot to tell you these are the only four areas you need to focus on in this phase. And nothing else is more important if you are just into the business. As you know, marketing and sales are for increasing revenue, and operation is about concentrating on delivering the right quality product at the right time. And finally, the finance is where you make a budget for each of those other two areas mentioned above. I also know the budget will not be that proper in most of the startups. Especially in online business, all you care about is the cost of setting up a store. Have you started the business just now? Then, I would suggest you guys to only focus on these four business functions. Once you acquire customers, you should scale the business (that is the scaling phase) and hire management teams to take care of these biz functions and some of the others along with it. The scaling phase is where you build teams to achieve your business goals. But this book is written to help the internet entrepreneurs who are into the setting phase right now. If that is the case, I urge you to focus only on marketing, sales, operations, and finance.

Rome was not built in a day

Building a strong relationship with the customers will create a great bond and trust. But it can't be done overnight, at the same time it can be destroyed overnight. The customers must trust you and your business. If not, you won't get your sales online.

Trust is very mysterious and elusive. Also, the thing is, you can't fake it. But you could earn the trust of the target audiences by delivering more value than expected. I call it a "10 times more value" than the competitors. If your competitors in the market are already providing "10 times more value", then make it 20x. That's how you should build trust with the customers.

For the entrepreneurs who just started the business will have only one concern, that is their sales. No one will give me one million dollars if I tell them about my products. For that, I need to provide value for them through my free content or product giveaway to make the target customers trust me and do business with me for a million dollars. Also, feedback increases great trust in online business. If you want to make the first sale, then give away your products for free of cost and ask them for feedback. And advertise that to other customers. I call this "building trust by providing value." It will not stop from there, you need to provide continuous value once they become your regular customers. People will believe social proofs and start to buy the products only if they trust them. We care about someone we value and love people who care so much. Apply the same principle in business, always care about your customers, and they will love you more, and it will help to build a great brand online.

The whole picture – The Right Way

When I was studying at college, I got a chance to conduct a study on the cleaning services companies in the United Arab Emirates. Because from there I came to know the importance of the whole picture concept in the business. It is none other than understanding the market, industry, and business. It does not matter in which country you are in right now and it doesn't matter where you want to start a business.

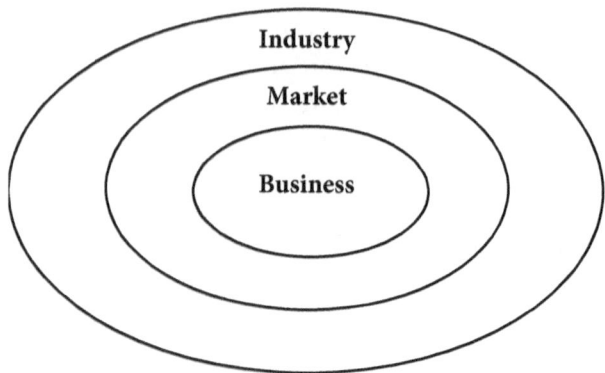

Fig. 1 The Whole Picture Concept

The first and foremost thing for you is to choose the business you want to play in. I will tell you now itself choosing the products first to sell online is not important. That's The Wrong Way. And, of course, selecting the specific market segment as your niche in that whole market segment is the immediate next thing. And finally comes the product or service you want to sell. From a brand perspective, you must have to select a category to go into the minds of the target customers and we will see that in a while.

Let's take an example: If you have been to the emirate of Dubai, you might have seen lots of cleaning company adverts and vehicles on the roads. I liked their work because they reduced the stress of working families (husband & wife), and clear the garbage in the homes. They acted as an extra arm to them. But it doesn't matter here and do you know what matters most? You guessed it correctly! It is the lesson. The cleaning services market has many segments, like residence cleaning, company cleaning, sewage cleaning, etc. You already know choosing the market you want to be in is the second step. When you know the business you want to be in, then it means you also know the market partially. The next step is selecting the specific market niche in that whole market segment to play in.

Let's assume you have decided to go on with the residence cleaning, and that will be your market segment. And you can still drill down to select a specific market niche in that chosen market segment. In this case, you help the working families (hubby and wife) by doing their household chores. And that is the service you offer to your target customers. We will be seeing more about target customers in the upcoming chapter. If the business, market, and offer (product or service) are known, then the next step is the important one as you should categories the brand in the minds of the customers. Are you sure? Only your brand should be in that category in your market. That's where value proposition and uniqueness come in, and we will be seeing it later briefly.

For example, if a brand is known for its safety, then they should have placed themselves in the safety category before the competitor. And meanwhile, you might have seen a brand positioned in luxury. Likewise, you have to categories your brand in the minds of the target customers. If you categorize the brand in quality, then you should do that first before the competitors. If not look for other categories. I hope you now have a fair idea about the whole picture concept, and I tell you what? It is inevitable for any business. All successful companies would be in some category and it is time for you to do the same.

The value redefined

Internet entrepreneurs should identify the pains of the customers and give a solution for that pain. Without understanding the customers you can't sell the products. That's why most online businesses fail. If the marketplace already has the same products as yours. Ask yourself this question: Why should customers buy from you? If your competitors are also selling the same products, then you are one among the player playing the same game in the same category. How come customers choose you in the first place? It is based on uniqueness. I think anyone can guess it and your products should offer unique value to the customers.

Always analyze the pain points of the customers. If any pain points are missed by the competitors? Great! That is where you must concentrate. The Harvard professor Theodore Levitt once said that *"people don't buy a quarter-inch drill, they want a quarter-inch hole."* You can't sell the products by defining the features and benefits (product attributes) alone. Even though you have the correct target customers list. That's the old way of doing, and many are still doing the same. I tell you what? It will never improve your sales.

Asking questions will always lead to correct answers. You need to ask, what customers are expecting the product to do? You will get a different insight and that's where your value proposition lies. For sure, if you approach business this way, the sales will increase gradually. The business should create value for target customers. It is not possible if you do not understand them. And you should discover: what they expect from the product? what are their pain points, desire, frustration? Then only you can create value by addressing those pain points and expectations of the customers regarding the product or service. Ask yourself: what job the product should do for the customers?

****Brainstorming Activity****

****Try to apply the principle with your products and analyze the results for yourself****

Consider you're selling chocolate shake. And you know it's one of the products which is available in all corners of the fast-food restaurants. If you define only its features and benefits like fresh milk or a healthy drink, it will not do you any favor. Instead, try to figure out: what customers are expecting the product to do? You will get to know a different perspective like experience. You will get some insights: For example, the customers prefer to buy it because it is easy to take away. Also, it will be easy to have it while traveling. It is not like eating burgers and other food. Just like that, try to figure out the different perspectives of value you could define with your products. It is not about functional benefits alone, instead, it is of emotional and self-expressive benefits too.

****Try this out to provide value to the customers ****

If you want to provide value to your customers, you first have to understand them by talking to them. It can be done through interviews, surveys, or a little phone conversation can also help to understand them. Just find out what is most important to them and try to serve well in that. But it will not happen if you don't know how to do it. Try to create "10 times more value." It should be 10 times the value of the product minus the cost of the product. Different people have different needs, and they perceive value based on that. So, it's better to choose one target customer to serve their needs. Because the product attribute may be attractive to one customer segment and may not be appealing to others. Therefore, the entrepreneurs need to analyze what is most important to one or a few target customer groups in their market and utmost try to fulfill them. The main goal is to create a win-win situation. It is possible by providing value for customers to make them happy and maximize sales. Because happy and satisfied customers will always pay more and buy repeatedly. Just try to focus more on the valuable customers and try to wow them through your offers and deliver them quickly.

Know the essentials, wishes, & insistence

I want entrepreneurs to understand human essentials, wishes, and insistent. End of the day, you are going to sell the products to humans. That's why I think it is vital to understand their essentials, wishes, and insistence to better your product offerings in the marketplace than the competitors. I love the concept of Maslow called the hierarchy of human needs. But we are not going to look at that now. Although, I wish you to have a look at it. Your products should fall into any of these categories. It could be either essential or wish. If it is not both, then it should be insistent. If your product falls in the essentials category, then it would be unavoidable for human survival like food, water, clothing, shelter, education, and healthcare. It doesn't require a push in the marketplace. But in today's scenario, even these category products need to be promoted because of the competition. And needs category is not only physical but also there for social needs like belonging, affection, and individual needs like knowledge and self-expression.

The child needs milk but it wants candy

The next thing which leads us to look at the wishes. And it is not a permanent thing first, and it will always change over time. It is because of individual culture and personality. We don't need a good smelling shampoo to take bath, but still, we like it. Thus, the product falls in the wish category is a not mandatory part of our life. The individual's social and personality preferences are the deciding factor. The wish category changes as time passes. Unlike essentials, wish is not necessary for survival, but if the customers manage to satisfy the wish, then it turns into essentials. I put in this way, a lot of the products in today's world falls in the wished category because we don't need Coco-cola, Starbucks, and iPhone to survive.

Creating demand is very hard but filling it is not

If anyone falls in the insistent category, then they will be ready to buy the product for a premium price. They would be your high-end customers because these are the individuals who want premium products and they could also buy them. If that is the case, they are seeking to convert their wishes into insisting. The only difference between wishes and insistence is desire. If someone desires something but do not have the money to buy it, then they can't fulfill the desire. The customer wants BMW, Mercedes, or prefers the iPhone over Samsung. For all these things desire plays an important role to convert that into insistent. And it is backed up by the buying power of the people.

A connection is not a communication

There is a quote: A business with better communication with the customers win. It would be a key take away for modern businesses today. The traditional customer communication is seeking out the way in the marketplace. To better their relationship with the customers which helps a lot in making them repeated buyers. A smart entrepreneur knows it very well that making a new customer is hard because it consumes time and money. Instead, he will make the already acquired customers buy from him repeatedly. It will be an effective way. Many online businesses have social media accounts on different platforms. But the question is: Are you connecting with the target customers? If they follow you on social media it does not mean they are interested in building a relationship with you. Most often, the entrepreneurs never thought of talking to their followers.

I think from there the downfall starts. And I must agree with one thing here. Without understanding the customers, you can't make efforts to build a relationship with them.

Effective communication is the key to success. As it helps to know your target customer needs in and out so that you can create value through the content you post online. Think of building a relationship with a stranger next to your home who got shifted recently. No one will deny this because it will start with the communication to know their needs so that you can also take part in helping them. It will create trust and give a great first impression. That is very important in building a great relationship, but you should do it consistently to engage with anyone. Just apply the same stuff in business and see how it helps to build a relationship with the target customers. It will increase sales, make them buy repeatedly, and refer you to their families and friends.

Employee v/s Entrepreneur mindset

One of the most common reasons for the failure of the online business is the people who wish to start a business with an employee mindset. If you want to be an entrepreneur then think like one. As far as I could see, many online businesses failed because some people had a paycheck mentality. They wanted to get success in business that is so good, but they failed to think like an entrepreneur and lacked beyond in their mindset. Entrepreneurs are the one who takes some risk, think big, and have never given up attitude even if they fail. On the other hand, people with an employee mindset seek security with the investment they intended to make and they won't make them come out of their comfort zones. That is why they never take any risks. Also, they give up sooner without a fightback right after the downfall in the business. They mostly wish to play safer. I promise you it will not help you to make big cash. The paycheck mindset is not a thing you wish to go for while starting a business. I have seen many people with an entrepreneur mindset never ask anyone to catch the fish for them. They learn how to catch the fish from the one who has done it already and do it for themselves. It does not matter to them even if they fail miserably. They just try until they succeed. Everyone knows the thinking of a successful person differs from the mediocre or unsuccessful one. If you want to be successful in business, then think like super-rich or successful people in any field. You will know that is not the way most people think, and it will be different in all aspects.

What is your role now?

There are two things you as an entrepreneur should keep in mind. The first one is the market you are going to play in. The second one is the product that you are going to sell because you should decide something important here. Do you want to disrupt the market with your solution? Are you planning to sell what others are already selling in the market place slightly better than the competitors? You should have that clarity before you go for the online business stuff. In my opinion, the latter would be the best choice for you to go along with some passion. It helps to build your brand online because most of the businesses in the world revolve around it. But don't think that I am not a fan of market disruption. It is the need today. Because innovation is a must for entrepreneurs to go on. Even if they start with the latter one, the earlier one (Market Disruption) should the end goal for them to attain in the future. As I said, first identify the needs of the target customers and secondly offer products to satisfy it. Most online businesses fail because all they care about is a product. And having a mindset that they can sell anything through Facebook and Google ads without understanding the customer needs. That's called working in The Wrong Way. As I mentioned before, everyone should take the business seriously to win. Because there is no short-term goal in business. Always think long term! That's why the failure rate is so astounding because starting an online business is very easy, but earning a profit is not. If you don't love what you do, then it is not going to go in your way anymore. Now, it is time to move on to the next chapter. So, let's dive deeper to look at the factors that affect online business in the start-up phase. And you are going to learn how to choose a market niche for your business along with an interesting story. See ya there!

CHAPTER – 2

"Entrepreneurs are not planned to fail but they failed to plan" – Anonymous

A Horror e-commerce story

The internet gave birth to many online companies in the last '90s because of the massive growth in the usage and adaptation of the dot com. So many companies were seen on the internet, but a lot of companies failed bigger and only a few companies are standing tall even today. We are going to see one such company that had so many expectations while starting. The company was named boo.com. The boo.com is considered to be one of the biggest failures of the dotcom burst. It happened almost two decades ago. But still, we are talking about this online sports clothing company. Because it is a lesson for all start-ups marketing. Boo.com was founded in the year 1998. The founders of boo.com were already millionaires. They sold their bookselling website called bookus.com before starting boo.com. The boo.com was the first online sports retailer had more than 100 branches all over the world. It was closed in the year 2000. Because it could not raise funds further from the investors. Let's have a look below to find out what went wrong.

Marketing a product that was not carefully planned

The boo.com decided to create awareness for more than 350,000 potential customers, even before going online. They started marketing even before developing their site. The millions of dollars lavishly spent on advertising campaigns for the brand that yet to be gone live. It took a long time to develop the site, but marketing expenses were on skyrocket without single sales.

Know the reality of the customers

The boo.com wanted to transfer the physical shopping experience to online to attract the target group of young people. They developed the virtual assistant called the Boo. The boo guided customers who visited the website to make their shopping experience ease online. This software was a bit complex to develop. It worked only on broadband connections, but most of the people used the dial-up connections at home those days. The customer who visited the boo.com website had to download bulk software. They even waited for 8 seconds to complete the loading process, which eventually annoyed the customers.

Don't market for the sake of public relation

Boo.com marketing was heavily dependent on public relations. They spent an enormous amount on marketing. They produced a magazine named Boom and published in various languages. It sounds good, isn't it? But the problem emerged when they only competed with the fashion magazines of its kind. It didn't provide the opportunity to order the products of boo.com in any way possible. The separate catalog styled magazine had been produced for the existing customers to order the product. It made the brand widely known but with no improvement in sales results.

Lessons Learned

- The marketing should be based on the product.
- Know your customers well don't leave them behind by going ahead (If the customers are using dial ups don't give them something on broadband).
- Marketing should be related to and support sales.

Factors that affect online business in the start-up phase

"Quality is the best business plan" – John Lasseter

In 2015, some reports said that 70% of U.S. people shop online for at least a month. Still, most aspiring internet entrepreneurs believe that attractive designs, websites, and pricing is enough to be successful in e-commerce. But there are many factors to consider before jumping into the online business to avoid failure in the start-up phase. Many aspiring entrepreneurs fall into the trap of content, which shows e-commerce business like a cakewalk, but achieving overnight success is not everyone's game. If you think only about the product and Facebook ads are enough to be successful in online business, then you will fail for sure. That is what I call The Wrong Way. But you could ask me about the factors that affect the online business which is listed below. And that's how you should approach the business even before choosing the products in the first place. These factors are essential to start any business both online and offline also, it applies to any marketplace.

Factors that need to be considered

Entrepreneurs are not planned to fail, but they failed to plan as implementation is very important than strategies. The lack of planning made store owners failed to focus on specific necessary steps both before and after setting up an online store. Here are the factors that affect the online business in the start-up phase. Aspiring entrepreneurs need to consider these factors while thinking of setting up an online store in the future. Also, it might be helpful to correct their mistakes now, if they have one already as it will not be too late to refocus.

End to End Online business Knowledge

If you ask people who are already in online business, 100% entrepreneurs out there not only agree to the fact but also, they will tell you the importance of knowing the system you are going to play in. It is not mandatory to know everything top to bottom as most of the things can learn by staying up in the process. But still, it is somehow necessary to have some basic knowledge before jumping into the real game.

Insufficient Investment

The interesting thing about starting a business online is only a few hundred dollars away. For this reason, many people starting without proper prerequisites. Many aspiring entrepreneurs start the business online by investing the amount, but the problem comes when they fail to think beyond that. Doing business online also requires labor and capital like brick and mortar stores. A few hundred would be good to start, but entrepreneurs need to think about long-term objectives. It is advisable to plan the expenses for inventories and other requirements like marketing expenses which need investment frequently to make your sales start kicking. The poor marketing investment has shut the business after three to four months. They did not know what to do to kick start the sales lead to a horrible end.

Selling similar products

Another horrible mistake people often do while starting a business online is selling the same products. They sell similar products like competitors, which will drag them to failure. Every entrepreneur must think about why should customers buy from you, and what values are you providing more than your competitors? As I already mentioned in the earlier chapter, ask the question of why should customers buy from you? Still, you are selling similar products that are available in every brick and mortar store and even online? You should differentiate your business offerings to stand out. And position the products to be unique in the minds of the customers. It should give superior values to your customers than your competitors.

Lack of long term goals

Most entrepreneurs who fail in online business have many reasons, but this one is crucial they eventually had no long-term goals. Your intention and goals should play together for achieving success in online business. It will act as fuel to run any business for the long term. And it will give you an aim to achieve and plan to reach that level.

All strategic decisions to achieve the goals of your business has to be long term as it is not achievable in the short run. So, it is indeed worth it for entrepreneurs to have long term business goals to achieve successful results.

Develop products based on market needs

Customers don't buy products if they don't need it. All successful products should be developed based on the analysis. The product should solve customer needs because they will pay for products that meet their needs. Entrepreneurs should not build a product and look for the market to sell it. It is advisable to look for market requirements to develop any products. Most entrepreneurs who fail in online business mostly fall in the first category. You will fail even if you spend more bucks on marketing if you develop the product without knowing any needs of the customers.

Awareness about the market condition

It is indeed very crucial for entrepreneurs to know about the market they are inside. As it will help to identify the current trends in the market. Based on that entrepreneurs can use the opportunity to build their products and online business. It also will avoid entrepreneurs to develop something which already saturated in the market. It is very crucial to keep an eye on the market condition for a successful online business. Before jumping into the business, you must know about the demographics of that market and target audiences to tailor-made the products to suit that market needs.

Poor Marketing Strategies

Everyone will agree with me if I say marketing is the heart of the business. Without promoting the product, the potential customers will not know about your offers in the market. You should make awareness about the business to make sales and earn profit out of it. But the problem arises when entrepreneurs don't have proper strategies to market their products online. Keep in mind all you are doing is paying the marketers for the possibility of sales but not paying for actual sales. Most of the time, it will lead to zero sales and end up shutting the business. Social media is a middleman to market your products to the customers, but it will not be an overnight success. Firstly, the entrepreneurs need to create awareness about the product to develop interest among the customers to make them desire to purchase your product. It needs a lot of hustle and hard work to showcase your products to customers. But it will give success in the long run.

Pick a niche

Choosing a market niche is always a challenging task for internet entrepreneurs. Sadly, most aspiring entrepreneurs always think about the products that they want to sell when it comes to online business instead of the target market and business they want to do.

The correct approach is to choose an industry that you want to start a business and then drill down further to know the market. Most of the online businesses fail within a few months because all they think about is a product when it comes to starting a business. They also choose to serve the broad market segment which is impossible to fight with fierce competition.

In a pre-internet era, more often businesses used to market themselves as everything to everyone. Because customers find it difficult to search for a range of suppliers for the product. But things have changed drastically in the present scenario of the internet era where the customers can easily select different suppliers and the products by comparing the cost and quality. There will be no competitive edge in everything to everyone anymore. It would be appropriate to serve a specific group of customers instead of everyone, especially if you're starting an online business. The broader perspective will never help you anymore.

When starting a business online, many people think of Amazon and eBay.com. They have a variety of products portfolio. But the thing is when you are starting an online business, it will be difficult to gather such huge investments, and your marketing budget will skyrocket. Mostly, you would be the one-man army to do all the work from top to bottom. You won't have dedicated teams for different business functions. To achieve success entrepreneurs should follow the niche model. It is very well suited for starting a business online. I will also agree that selecting your market niche will be one of the very crucial aspects of online business. We will see it in more detail soon. As of now, I want to convey that focusing on a specific market segment will be a lot easier task while starting a business online. It will save you time and money.

Think tall but go short

It's not a bad idea to start with a narrow segment if you're first starting a business. The entrepreneurs don't have to stock a range of products or even think of it. The customers will pursue you as a niche specialist in the chosen market. There are a lot of chances available to make a business deal with you instead of generic suppliers as you become the first point of contact. Also, they will pay you a premium price for the products if you develop a brand.

Starting small will make you focus on a single product idea to enter the market and expand way going forward. You can relate that with most successful companies today.

They should have had one single product while entering the market. They expanded it further to explore other markets internationally with a diverse product portfolio. They also made the same product based on the needs of the market. The main drawback of choosing the broader segment will make the entrepreneurs increase the advertisement cost as well. Instead, selecting a narrow segment will make these costs lesser and helps to charge a premium price for the product. More importantly, it will make them handle fewer customers.

Let's take an example: if you are planning to sell pet products online that include both cats and dogs. As you know, there are a lot of competitors available for this market. And it is flooded with cats and dog products online. Your point of survival is thin to compete with big and established competitors. Thus, it would be reasonable to select a narrow segment (A specific dog or cat breed category) in ay market niche. It will shrink the competition and it will make you a niche specialist.

Choosing a market niche

What would be the most frustrating moment in starting an online business other than selecting a profitable niche? Now, it's time to explore the right niche for you. It is none other than knowing your skills, passion, and the demand in the marketplace. As always, the right questions will give perfect answers to you. The potential market niche can be based on your profession. It would be from your hobbies too. Or it could be from your industry and social group. Finally! It could also be on the past and present physical habits.

Ask questions to yourself and look at your resume and analysis your experience, activities, and try to find suitable answers. That could be your MARKET NICHE for your online business. If you're not passionate about what you're doing, then it won't last long. It is very important to choose the market niches based on your passion and interest. The fact here is you should enjoy doing it as a business, and you should put every hard work into it. Even, for some time you must tolerate everything. Sometimes it could be a slight downfall or failure. If you are passionate, it will make you run. Because you love doing it, and you always see the long-term growth of it. As always, it is easier to fill the demand than creating one. It is also very much acceptable to create products based on your area of expertise, interest, or passion. It will make you easily understand the needs of the customers to provide the solution.

It's simple, be a member of your target market. So that you can easily understand their needs by being one of them. Also, it is vital to choose a narrow market segment and dominate it instead of going broader. It reminds me of the bestselling author and entrepreneur Tim Ferris's quote, it goes like this "Be the big fish in the small pond." The entrepreneurs should keep in mind that being a small fish in the big pond does not make sense because you would be destroyed by the fierce competition that already exists in the market. So, it is wise to choose a single market niche and be a big fish in the small pond. Later, you can move on further to fight with all the big fishes in the ocean too.

CHAPTER – 3

"Implementation is important than strategies" –
Anonymous

A classic example of product development error

As you already know the dotcom bubble had given birth to several online companies in the late '90s because of the boom of the internet. The pets. com was an online company that sold pet-related supplies to customers. It was founded in 1998 and got shut down in the year 2000, the company operated at the headquarters in San Francisco, USA, at that time. Amazon had a 30% stake in this company. Amazon was one of the few companies which survived the dot com burst in the early 20s. Pets. com had almost 320 employees, and I would say it was a humble beginning. Pets.com got its name because of the sock puppet advertisement. And the famous slogan which said: "Pets.com because pets can't drive." Pets.com was seen to be successful in the year 1999, although it did not last long. It had raised $82 million through IPO in 2000 approximately nine months before the shutdown. According to Wolverton, pets.com hoped to become the one-stop-shop for pet supplies and had planned to offer a wide range of pet products than any of its competitors including products carrying labels. They also collected money from investors for marketing and distribution.

The key issues

Pets.com had several issues that contributed to the failure of the business. Firstly, it failed to differentiate its product from the competition. It sold similar products that were available in all online pet stores and even in brick and mortar stores. All they pursued was a low-cost strategy for selling their products to consumers with no differentiation strategy to place their products in some category in the minds of customers. It also entered the market by selling the lower price pet foods and supplies. But it made the cost huge on shipping which was unaffordable to the customers. The problem occurred when they did not investigate the customer's desires. Because they tended to purchase pet items in discount stores while shopping for their needs.

The main thing was, it took a lot of time to ship the product to the customers, but they did not want to wait to receive the product. It made them feel great inconvenience. The storage cost was also the factor because pets.com did not work well on the place strategy. These unsold products were in the warehouse and it made them lose a huge chunk of money in operating expenses. This forced the company to relocate the warehouse from San Francisco to cut the cost.

They lowered the cost of the product to capture the market share but failed to concentrate on profitability. It made them spend more money on marketing and reduced the cost of the product. They also sold lesser than the actual buying price. The pets.com just developed the product and tried to sell it without any research about the target customers and their actual needs. And it led to the failure of the famous dot-com bubble company. As you know that advertisement is the tool to showcase the business offerings to the target customers. Both success and failure of the companies will also depend on it.

Why pets.com failed?

"If you are not embarrassed by the first version of your product, you've launched too late." –
Reid Garrett Hoffman

Pets.com was indeed a dot-com disaster, there was plenty of companies came out with high expectations, but it did not live up to the dream. If we analyze the fact, we can see that product development would be the main reason behind it. The first lesson pets.com taught is to develop the product based on the target customer's needs. For that, you have to do market research so that companies can understand what customers really want in that marketplace. Also, the product should solve the problem of the customers. The Pets.com also taught the importance of being unique and to be perceived in some categories in the minds of the customers. If any competitors are already serving the market with a similar product, then we should differ. If the competitor was selling the same pet products, then pets.com should have differentiated its brand to the customers. Pets.com had failed to position it well. As a result, customers perceived the pets.com brand the same as competitor brands. Pet's.com failed to add value to the customers.

Insane Marketing Approach

Pets.com spent almost $300 million in less than two years before folding. They burnt 1.2 million dollars on an advertising campaign to build the brand around the sock puppet. It indeed created a lot of awareness for the customers, but soon the management realized some issues. There was a demand for the products, but they were nowhere near to the expectation. The campaigns created a lot of awareness with a little bit of interest to them, but there was no desire and action among the customers. There was no need for home delivery on those days. Most people had shown interest in buying pet supplies at brick and mortar stores while doing the shopping for their needs. As a result, the awareness made through advertising attracted only a few customers to buy the products. It teaches the importance of knowing the needs of the customer. And selling similar products the same as competitors wouldn't help you as well. The pets.com should have differentiated themselves from the competition. This tells clearly: if there is no need for the product, then spending a lot of money on marketing does not do any favor. It would create awareness and some interest among the customer, but they won't desire to take action to buy the product if it is not needed.

Lessons Learned

- Market analysis is a must before developing any products.
- Even massive marketing campaigns will not help companies if there is no need for the product. It will create awareness and interest but not turned out to be a desire and action.
- Selling similar products, the same as competitors without any uniqueness, will never help the company. On the other hand, it will fold without any sales.

- Know the buying behavior of the target customers.
- And see whether they search online or offline.
- It will help companies to sell their offerings.
- Remember to position the company uniquely in the minds of the customers in some categories.
- The customers should perceive your brand differently among competitors.

Effective Online Business Marketing Strategies Checklist

The one thing that frustrates internet entrepreneurs while thinking of doing business online or after setting up an online store is none other than formulating effective marketing strategies to generate traffic on the site to capture leads.

A recent study refers that 89% of respondents feel that email is generating more leads. Followed by content marketing and search engines. Nearly 93% of the leads generated from these three online channels alone. They are website referrals, direct traffic, and search engines. Before spending bucks on advertising to generate traffic and leads. Entrepreneurs should know some things that are considered as very crucial for the success of the online business. I can say that effective marketing for any business starts with these checklists. We are now going to discuss below. If entrepreneurs spend their marketing budget without considering these checklists, then it would be nothing but a waste of resources and time.

These checklists are a prerequisite to designing effective marketing strategies for any online business. Mostly, Entrepreneurs start with marketing straightaway to promote their business. But to get success, there are a few most inevitable processes that need to be taken care of before designing effective marketing strategies for all online businesses.

Know your market

Entrepreneurs should know their business market in and out to build a sustainable business online. If don't, then you would not be in the business. You must explore the market by testing it so that you can know about the latest trends in it. Without a proper understanding of the market, it will cause the business to fail even if you spend a lavish amount on marketing the products to the customers. Always develop the products based on the needs in the market. Another most important thing is to analyze the macroenvironmental elements in the market. Such as political, economic, social, technological, legal, and environmental factors to keep an eye on changing market conditions.

Competition

Another thing the entrepreneurs must know to succeed in the online business is none other than understanding their competitors in that market in which it is running. Entrepreneurs should know about the competitors products (already available in the market), customers, and marketing strategies. With that insight, you can develop the marketing strategy of your company with something better to standout.

Product Research

Developing the products based on the customer's need is the secret recipe for success. The business should not develop the products and look for the market to sell it. The product should be developed based on customer requirements. Most businesses develop products without knowing the target customer needs, which is the wrong way. It is the single most important reason for the failure of the online business. Entrepreneurs should always try to solve the problem through the product. Hence, the product research will help the entrepreneurs to understand the customer's needs.

Customer Buying Behavior

Internet entrepreneurs are recommended to understand customer buying behavior to know where they buy the product that you are selling. It will help the entrepreneurs to know which products to sell online. If there is no need for customers to buy online, then what is the point of selling those products through online channels? By knowing the customer behavior, it will help the entrepreneurs to write great product descriptions to stress out the points that motivate the customers to make a purchase decision. Understanding their activities, interests, opinions will help the entrepreneurs to target more precisely.

Effective Marketing

As always, marketing strategy involves two key questions: Which customers you are going to serve? (Segmentation and Targeting) and How to create value for them? (Positioning & Differentiation). Understanding the target customer is a must for any online business. If you understand one group of target customers in the beginning it will be helpful for effective marketing. It makes you know who will buy your product in those demographics. The differentiation and positioning of the brand in some categories will make you stand out in the market. Remember, selling similar products like competitors will drag you to fail miserably.

Create a brand

Every internet entrepreneur should think about creating a brand. The brand is not just a logo. It is much larger than that. Your brand is a value and it is a sum of experience you deliver to the customers. The brand is a promise you deliver to the customers. To build a great brand, every entrepreneur should know who they are (For what they stand for) and what value they are bringing to the customers. You are selling the ideas, not the product. As mentioned earlier, it should differentiate from the competition. It is better to focus on small communities rather than everyone else (in the beginning). Everything will start to grow organically because it will take at least three years to build a brand and reputation. Consistency is the key to build a strong brand online.

Offering

Internet entrepreneurs should be very keen on offering unique products on the market. Product research is very important to develop products based on market needs. It helps to offer great products in the market without developing similar products like competitors. It should also satisfy the needs of the consumers and offer superior value. A clear understanding of the product will make you successfully promote it to the customers. As it will not happen without concrete knowledge of the product the entrepreneurs intend to sell.

Pricing

I love the pricing part of the business and I hope everyone will love it without having a second thought about it. Pricing will decide your business success, and entrepreneurs need to understand the target audience to set the price of the product. Keep in mind the price and quality are directly proportional. Also, you should focus on selling, delivery price, and production costs to set the price of your product. So, the entrepreneur should understand the impact of pricing as it will reflect on profit margin, supply, demand, and marketing strategies.

Advertising

You got the product and decided the price to sell in the market, and now it is time to promote it to potential customers. The promotion of the product will require differentiation of the product information to the consumers. There are certain elements needed to promote the product to the customers. It can be through advertising, public relation, affiliate marketing, online marketing, etc. But it should be done based on your target audience. If your target customers are the people around 45 years of age, then there are chances that they won't use much of an online platform. As an entrepreneur, you need to go for advertising based on your target customer's congregation and it could be both offline and online or any of the ones.

Influencer Marketing

Entrepreneurs have a great option to promote their brands to customers. Yes, with the help of a strategic deal between the influencers in their niche on social media. It is very much possible to promote and to educate potential customers to make awareness about your products easily without any hustle and much effort. This approach will provide a great return on investment, but the only challenge is to find better influencers in your niche to get success in the long run.

Place

The Internet is providing opportunities for aspiring entrepreneurs to sell products online, and it empowers the business to go international. The business which runs on the internet is no longer local anymore. The business owners need to know the place to sell the right product at the right price at the right time. So, entrepreneurs should know where the customers are buying or looking for the products which you're selling. It will be inappropriate if you are selling the product online and the potential customers are looking for it in brick and mortar stores.

How to do Market research

Entrepreneurs can research the market in several ways. You can call the customers in that market and talk to them to get to know them better and their needs. So that you can give the solution to their problems. You can also conduct the face to face interviews with the customers or survey online to get the information from them. Nowadays, you could also simply observe the customer's activities on Facebook and Instagram easily. But you must use these techniques based on the marketplace. Why is that? In some cultures, people feel annoyed if you call them but they will be ok for F2F interviews. Just know what to do before applying any of these techniques.

You can do market research by these two methods. The first one is called field research and that's the primary market research. And another one is the desk research and that's the secondary method. In the present scenario, you can easily collect the data through desk research with the help of Google. And search the information needed for those demographics. Once you get the customers, you can get the data through field research, but that needs a little bit of hustling to start in the beginning. Always remember to research on a regular interval. To get to know the market, current trends, and customer buying behavior. Because if you neglect, then you can't survive in the business for a long time. Since the business environment is ever-changing and if you are not up to date then you will easily be driven away from the competition (See Nokia's story). Therefore, entrepreneurs need to know the market for successfully running the business online.

Who is your customer & where do they reside?

The only thing that is of great significance while starting an online business is none other than knowing who is your potential customer and where do they reside? If you do that correctly, then it will be a golden ticket for your business success. Many aspiring entrepreneurs are thinking their business is for everyone. And I would surely tell you that this will be a path to failure. Don't believe me still? Then I recommend you to go through chapter 2 again. Even the generic description of customers will be equally deceiving. So that I want you to narrow the focus like a laser on one specific target customers. Just jump and know what their interest is, what activities do they like the most, what are their frustrations, etc. Gather all the information as much as you could But here is the catch! Some people will wait to get to know the full info. And I will tell you it is like measuring the depth of the ocean.

You probably can not make it for sure. Therefore get going is the best way to know target customers and their needs in the market. If you wait to know everything, then you would lose the game. You can also ask people from your target market by conducting a quiz, collaborating on social media to build a relationship with them. Also, you can use any online platform to know them better while doing your regular things. Because it is not going to end as far as you are in the business. Think about your whole market segment as a community. And start to know them better by staying in the process. There will always be a category that is leftover or unnoticed by the rivals and competitors in your marketplace.

I want you to focus on that specific category and become a leader on that to make it unattractive to the competitors. We can take the dog products for example. We know there are many dog-related products in the market all over the world. If not, I am sure, it will be there at least in your marketplace. And you can't compete with well-established brands of that specific niche. As I mentioned earlier, it will be like small fish in the big pond. The dog market already has a lot of competition. And your voice will not have sound if you choose to go on with the same niche and category.

So, I want you to go on and sell the product for the specific dog breeds because it will make you a niche specialist in that category. And can easily become a big fish in that small pond. Keep in mind, build a strong brand around some category (Positioning) and make the competitors irrelevant for that. Importantly, don't forget to quote the premium price. To do all of these, you should first choose the segment you want to be in and find out where the target customers are congregating in social media. You already know I always believe that correct questions will give the correct answers. Yeah, you found that! You need to ask yourself some questions to know who is the target customers & where are they residing?

Who is my target customer?

To find out who is your customer, you need to separate them by answering these questions. Firstly, find out who is your target customer, where do they live, what he/she passionate about, what are their goals, desire, and dreams. If you find answers to these questions, you will know your customers. But that would be the first step, and the second step is where are they residing? But before going into that, I want to pay more attention to this part with an example.

Most online entrepreneurs won't give importance to segmenting their customers and that mistake will make them not knowing their target customers. To find this, I want you to identify the customers based on personal characteristics like age, gender, income level, ethnic background, and education level. Entrepreneurs can find many different characteristics with the help of social media if you want to dig deeper and not so interested in traditional demographic segmentation. You can find some juicy information like what is their favorite movie, their hobbies, etc. And which posts do they like, comment, and share, etc. They want a message that directly speaks to them. If not, they will ignore you. Because they are scrolling loads of information per day on social media and ignore if it does not apply to them. That's why most Facebook ads will not perform as you think. Because the message is not relevant to them, and it does not address their concerns and pain points. But don't worry! We will see that more in detail later (in chapter 6).

So next time, if you worry that your ads are not performing as you think, then tweak the message that is appealing to the target market. But for that, you need to know your target customers very well. You should understand the pain points, passion, frustrations, their desires, what they search online. What phrases they search for, what magazines they read, would give some idea about your target customers. As an entrepreneur, you must find the answers to these questions. It will make you understand who your customers are. And it is your responsibility so that you can personalize your message to them and make them click your Facebook ads or any advertisements. The thing is if you find who your customer is, then you can easily find their desires, passion, dreams. You can also find how do they look and their goals easily if you make some extra effort.

Tips: Create a customer avatar using the above information and paste it on your wall.

Where do they reside?

If you decide on your customers, then the next step is to find where do they gather. For example, if you want to sell a product for school goers, then where do you find them? I think you guessed it right! It's at school. Apply the same principle here, but the only thing all you are going to do is finding the person mostly on social media like Facebook and Instagram. Also, it purely depends on your target customers. If your target customers are using Facebook there is no point in advertising on LinkedIn. Ask these following questions and try to find the best answers for them 1) Where do they hang out 2) If they are in social media, then which they part of 3) What articles do they read 4) What interest do they have 5) What posts do they read on social media. Consider if your target customers are online entrepreneurs, then you need to find out the Facebook groups which they belong to, and they can read articles about marketing and online business mostly on sites like Entrepreneurs or Huffington posts to build their business. This is how you can find the gathering of the target customers. That's it! Now, you know who your target audience is and where do they reside. It is time for you to implement it in your business.

Finding target customers

If you find out who your customer and where do they reside, then finding the target customers is not a hectic job. Go to Google and type the relevant keywords + Forum.

For example, if you are intended to sell the yoga products just go to Google.com and then type "Yoga Forum" to find what your potential customers are doing there. And, understand their needs by talking to them and you can target the forum to advertise your products. If you are not a Google person like me, then go to Facebook and type Group + Keyword in the search tab. Eventually, you will get all the groups in which your target customers reside. And you can build a relationship with them by asking for their needs and problems.

If you are too shy to ask, then conduct a survey or create a poll. First, you need to interact well in the group and earn their trust. It won't work if you right away sell your product there. Remember, Facebook groups are just for understanding customer needs and problems. You must target the audience in the Facebook ads, not directly in the groups until you build trust. The next question is: what are their passion and pain? If you interact with the group for a while, you can understand them. But you should be in the group as a member. Because some groups are a closed group and entertain only its members. You can easily find their passion and pain by looking into their social media posts, comments, pages they like, hobbies, etc by looking at their profiles.

If you do these things correctly, you can easily understand the target customer needs and try to provide value through your products by addressing their exact words in the Facebook ads which they talk in comments or the posts. For example, if your target customer is an online entrepreneur who will have issues in marketing the products to their customers. If you have a solution to their pain points, then you can use their exact words in the ad copy. And you can also advertise through FB ads by targeting the pages they like, activities, and interest. They will CLICK IT! The chances are more they will end up buying the product from you.

Perception & Uniqueness of your brand

How do you make your brand unique in the minds of the customers? It must stand out from the competition in the crowded marketplace. It is possible if you make the customers perceive your brand uniquely. For that, you should have to position your brand in some category in the minds of the customers. Positioning is not about playing with products (Uniqueness), but it is the art of playing with the customer's minds called the PERCEPTION. Entrepreneurs must differentiate the brand in the customer's mind. Again, if you find the answers to these questions, it would be helpful. Those are: What customers think of your brand? And how you want the customers to think about your brand? Not only that, but it is also to identify the ways to get into the customer's mind and hang in there. You want to know how? (See the Value redefined in CHAPTER 1). It will be done through the value proposition and knowing for what customers want the product to do and then understanding the pain of the customers because the uniqueness of the brand starts with positioning.

The top brands in the world seek ways to become first in the mind of customers in some categories, that's why they succeed so well and stand out on top. Think about Volvo, their value proposition is all about safety. Ferrari's value proposition is speed even though both Volvo and Ferrari are in the same industry still chose to be in a different category when it comes to occupying the minds of the customers. It makes one value proposition unattractive to another and helps to dominate the marketplace in that specific category. You know what? It will be a relief from market saturation. Likewise, it is vital to brand your business in some specific category if you want to be on top of the customer's mind. It will make competition irrelevant and unattractive.

Final thoughts

Effective marketing strategies for any online business should start with knowing the market, customers, and competition. The main thing is to develop a product by understanding the needs of the customers. That will be The Right Way because you need to know all these so-called business prerequisites to succeed in online business. And, remember that your product and Facebook ads alone cannot give you sales. It's called The Wrong Way. You can't neglect these areas and directly sell products to customers with the help of marketing. If the base is not well suited, then spending money on advertising will never help you. And it will lead to zero sales and shutting the business. So, it is vital to keep an eye on these areas to effectively design the marketing strategies for building any successful online brands. PERIOD!

CHAPTER – 4

"Don't find customers for your products, find products for your customers" – Seth Godin

The setback of an online grocer

Business failures often teach us great lessons than successful ones. The small business needs to take the right steps to succeed in the long run. To support that claim, we will look at Webvan's story as it was one of the biggest failures of the dot-com bubble ever. The Webvan was founded in the year 1999 by Louis and his brother tom. The investors had invested $3.5 million in his company as a benchmark capital.

Louis also obtained another $150 million from the other investors like yahoo. It made them move the company to IPO and helped them to raise another $375 million. Their new company already had $1.2 billion in the capital. That is great, isn't it? Board members and the top executives saw this as a tech company, not just as an online grocer. They thought that online grocery will offer greater convenience if they provide a wide variety of the product for 5% cost lesser than traditional stores. They also planned to deliver the purchased product for free of cost within 30 minutes. No surprise that Webvan had burned almost a billion dollars before shutting the business exactly two years after launch.

Mistakes of the Webvan

The end to end business knowledge

The biggest mistake of Webvan had done by the founders as well as the executives who had no previous hands-on experience in the grocery industry. The grocery industry is one of the smallest profit margin businesses with 1% to 2% of sales. At one point, the company needed sales of $103 per person to survive in the business in the year 2000. But the company expenses were $1.8 million, and sales were just $489,000.

Failed to understand the needs of the customers

Webvan didn't do any market research to understand the needs of the customers. They would have known it if they had done any group polls or surveys to see where the average customers go for grocery shopping and what is their needs. In the early '90s, many people wanted to pick their vegetables, fruits, and meats by themselves. People also used to select the items which were not on their list while doing shopping. Many customers preferred to buy items using discount coupons. But Webvan, on the other hand, didn't accept any coupons. And they didn't know that few customers were interested to save money by buying economy sizes. Those days, if a customer goes out shopping, they also preferred to it their clothes to dry cleaning, and some pick prescriptions while going out to the stores.

In the early stages of online exposure, the home stayed moms thought that people will say bad about them if they shop online, and did not buy groceries online. But that is not the case now. Webvan was not flexible because people had to order 24 hours in advance to get the items delivered. But usually, people preferred to change their lists at the last minute. And this did not favor busy working people and that worked against the Webvan.

Lesson Learned

- It is recommended to know the business in and out to get success.
- Market research is vital to know the customer's needs.

How well do you know your target customers?

The customers are an important aspect of the business. Whether it is online or brick and mortar stores. The whole objective of the marketing and sales would be to reach maximum customers to increase value and revenue. The customers buy the product or service to satisfy their needs. The product should satisfy the needs of the customers, not the needs of entrepreneurs. Have you ever been proud and happy about seeing your product listings on your store? It may feel promising to you, but the reality is the opposite. Have you ever surprised that why you haven't made any sales yet? Then, it is your topic because online entrepreneurs should have to understand the buying behaviors of individuals to sell the products or services. Customer behavior is none other than learning about human behavior in a customer role. Why is it vital for online entrepreneurs to understand customer behavior?

I would like to know where they prefer to buy the products that I am selling online. Because there is no point in selling the products online if the customers prefer to buy it in the brick and mortar stores. That's the deadliest mistake in online business. You know sooner or later the so-called online store will face a shutdown. The online environment has tons of products like yours. You ask yourself this question: why should customers buy from you? Does your product is available everywhere? Always remember that customers prefer to buy the products in well-established brands. If your so-called online store sells the same as them with no uniqueness, then, believe me, you won't make a sale for sure. That's why I stressed the importance of differentiation and positioning of your brand that appeals to the customers. The lesson we learned from one of the dot com bubble companies called the Webvan is simple. It indicates that if you don't understand the needs of the customers and their buying behavior, it will burst for sure. I don't want anyone of you to go through it, and that's the motive of this book. Let's jump and know what factors affect the customer's buying behavior.

The factor that affects customer buying behavior

Why should you know customer behaviors? You should not think that you can build customers easily. Just don't think: Hey! I have a beautiful online store, and the customers will love it. That attitude will be deceiving altogether, and the price will be huge to pay. I don't want to take that risk, neither you should. If so, here comes the answer, and it is nothing but just knowing how consumers make buying decisions for a product and based on what factors. We are the creatures of emotion. The factors are culture, social, personal, and psychological. If you mastered these four, then you likely understood the customer's buying pattern and behavior in the marketplace. That's a golden egg for any entrepreneurs. These four factors play a crucial role in consumer behavior, and it is the triggering point of the purchase on an exact product or service. Based on these four factors, they decide which product to pick or leave. If I say simply, it is vital for their decision-making process. They are conditioned by these four factors to make or break a deal. But I won't make you understand the boring definitions of these factors here. I prefer you to do it on your own to know it well. If you do it, then that would be much appreciable.

Customer buying blueprint

The customer's buying blueprint is a combination of thought, feeling, and action. When it comes to buying these four factors are used. They are cultural, social, personal, and psychological. These four factors are there for every individual, and it affects buying behavior. So, their childhood programming leads thoughts, and their thoughts lead to feelings, and their feeling leads to the final action to buy or reject the product based on the benchmark of these factors. It is stored in our minds and reflects whenever we buy the product as a customer. Without changing the program of these factors, buying behavior will not change. They will resist changing as well if they are deep-rooted in their cultural norms, social status, personality, and psychology. There are more chances that some of the consumers over prefer one factor than the other. In some cultures, it is of utmost importance and points all their actions based on one of these factors. Also, some will prefer social status over the other three factors, and some might give importance to personality and psych because it is purely dependent on the individual and the environment. Now, I believe you have got some clarity about the blueprint of customer buying behavior and understood the importance as well.

Why customers don't buy?

Have you ever surprised why the customer doesn't buy your product? Chances are more than they might have fallen into these five categories. Customer understanding does not stop after evaluating the factor that affects the buying decision. As an entrepreneur, you need to dig deeper to understand the buying process. Even if your brand is 100% unique from the competition. Still, customers do not buy if they do not need it now. If they have no needs, then they will not buy from you even if you provide a great product in the market. There is no possibility to buy now if they have already purchased the product. It is obvious they will not buy it now because their needs were satisfied by someone else in the marketplace. Sometimes customers also don't buy if they have no money. In some cases, the customers will have needs, but it will not reflect in a sale because they won't have money to fulfill that need. In another case, they will have money and need, but if it is not urgent now to buy it, then there are more chances that they won't buy.

That's why business always creates an urgency to make the prospects react quickly. There are more chances to make the purchase if they feel that they won't get it again if they take no action now. And it works well with one-time offers. Another thing is, if a customer finds another alternative product attractive to them, then they show no desire to buy it from you. The want factor does not work in your favor if they don't have the desire to buy. The last category is no trust, and this is where most businesses fall because the customers don't trust the businesses or entrepreneurs in the first go. Entrepreneurs must make the business trustable, and you already know Rome was not built in a day. It will take some time to build trust. And you have to make your brand stand out in the minds of the customers.

****Brainstorming Activity****

****Try it out yourself****

The first thing that customers do in making a buying decision is to recognize the need for that exact product or service to fulfill it. And it will be the first step. Different customers have different needs at different stages. As an entrepreneur, it is your responsibility to segment the target market and understand their needs to select one of them. If they recognize the needs, what could be the next step? That's right! They will search for information, and it could be online or offline. That's why I told you to know the target market because it is dependent on the target customers. Let's, for the sake of argument, assume that they look for information online. And there is no doubt they will GOOGLE it to find the products or services. Now, you can understand the importance of content marketing and SEO stuffs to rank for keywords in Google search results (Organically). You can place a bid on Google Ad-Words to show it on top whenever someone enters the keywords you had given (Inorganically). I know you might be delighted. But wait for a second because I will walk you through the next process. Customers are intelligent, and they don't buy a product or service on the first go. Because they will always have a plan B and search for other alternative products from the competitor brand to compare.

That is where brand choice plays an important role, and now you know why I highlighted positioning your brand in one category. Mostly, customers buy from the well-established brand unless someone close to them influences to try a different brand. Or there are possibilities that they buy different brands if they have no other choice in some situations. The post-purchase behavior is also an important one to look for because if they are not satisfied with the purchase they will prefer to go to some other brands. That is where the chances are more to buy your brand. But the only thing is to make sure that you fulfilled the expectations and the product's perceived performance. If you do these things correctly, you will earn trust and customer loyalty for your brand.

CHAPTER – 5

"An idiot with a plan can beat a genius without a plan" – Warren Buffett

How to Choose a Supplier?

Have you ever done dropshipping? Some people are starting an online business by watching attractive posts on Instagram and YouTube. A few self-proclaimed internet entrepreneurs and influencers on social media are telling people that doing business is everyone's cup of tea. Although, I believe success in business is only possible if we work based on the long term. Of course, you need other ingredients like hard work, persistence, and efforts. Because I started doing my first business by watching YouTube and Instagram posts that made business looks very easy and achievable. But the truth is very opposite to it because I chose the market I have never been to it before. I am not a cat person and I have no cats at home.

More importantly, I don't love cats that much, I neither like any pets. I had the mentality of selling anything to anyone through Facebook ads. The person who posted content on social media taught online business with pet products. No wonder! I followed the same thing, and end up broke.

Always choose the market niche based on your interest and skills. If not, you won't understand the needs and segmentation of the customers easily. Dropshipping has been the hottest topic in the online business for the last few years. Isn't it cool that you don't have to stock loads of products in the warehouse and don't have to ship the products to the customers? You can save the production, storage costs, and spend some of the few in marketing. All things will be taken care of by the third-party. That's great! But look again, this is where most budding entrepreneurs fall into the trap. I agree that dropshipping is a great business model. But you must follow some procedures and checklists to make it work. If not, it will be a disaster for sure. And the only good thing is you will end up spending a very few dollars on store setup and marketing, but nothing much in the products and storage before the closing ceremony.

Things to remember

As I said before, there are a few things that need to be taken care of before choosing the suppliers for your business. The suppliers are also one of the stakeholders who play a vital role in online business. If you consider doing dropshipping, then taking care of this area will reduce the 50% workload. You will be outsourcing product manufacturing and delivery to them. And you should have known the importance of that in online business, and that will be half of your headache. In my opinion, if you correctly handle this part, then you have no worries. But I want to open up something to you because this is not as easy as we talking about. I will also tell you that this might be time-consuming. And it will take its own time. Nobody can predict suppliers in the first place until you decided to test them on your own. You can also go on with the reputation of the suppliers in the marketplace if they are local, but the case is different for international suppliers (We will see it below). So, I believe time-consuming is a natural part of it.

When I first started my online store. I did not bother to choose the suppliers for my business, and most of the internet entrepreneurs won't do it either. All you do is load the website with lots of products and only care about the design of the website. And you will also make sure that it looks attractive and colorful. That will be the only concern when starting a business online for most of the people. I am not saying that these elements are not important. But there is a lot you missed out that is super important than this. And it will cause more trouble for your investment if you neglect. Before moving into the next part, I want you to follow me through this. The upcoming insight is not only for dropshippers but also for the entrepreneurs who wish to find the right suppliers for their business.

Don't find the right supplier they will be more of a partner

As you already know, the suppliers are one of the most important pillars in online business. If it is not well, then you can't deliver the right products to the customers at the right time. If the pillar is not strong, then you can't scale the business further. The problem is people don't bother about this and mostly handling it with the least care. It is because you might have not yet made your first sale online.

It is the reason most of the time. But imagine if you have made the first sale you have to deliver the products to the customers, then you will realize the importance of this pillar in your business. I will tell you a secret here, nobody will wait for long to get their package neither you nor me and nobody will. All of them expect to touch their ordered package sooner because we all hate waiting. You might ask me how to select the suppliers in the first place because they are all over in Ali express (If you are dropshipping) and both online and offline. Keep this in your mind: Don't just search for the right suppliers. I want you to find the right partners to help you with your business. I know it will be harder and there is no way. But remember, business is about hustling in the beginning. As you may hear of this saying which goes like "Don't give up because the beginning is always the hardest" sow the seed now, and I will tell you that the harvest will of worth. Okay, I know what are you thinking right now? How do you find one? That's fine! I am coming to that part now. There are some factors you should evaluate while finding the right supplier partners. Here it goes!

Fact: 1 – Earn the trust with the stakeholders

If you are searching for the supplier, your mindset should be to get a partner who helps to craft your business along with you. There will be mutual understanding and trust must be there between the stakeholders to do that successfully. The Right Way is to make the deal a win-win. It should benefit both the parties and done through talking with them. If anyone of you has hesitation, then it is best to drop it and make another deal until the agreement is acceptable on both ends to start with. It should be profitable for both of you. What do you think about the rejection of the proposal from suppliers most of the time? Mostly, the deal is not profitable to them.

If you approach a wholesale manufacturer of a product that you intend to sell, then try to make a deal using a win-win method (It should be profitable to both), and trust will increase over time. But you must be genuine being yourself. Try this! Send out an email or talk to them face to face if possible because it will make the work a lot easier. This is the first step if you earn the trust of the suppliers, and your burden will be half reduced in business. I understand what you are thinking right now. If you first approach the suppliers, their hand will be on the upper side. Especially if they are well established and standard suppliers in the market. It is not the case for everyone, at the end of the day all suppliers want to do business unless the deal is considered to be very small to them. But this is not an end, and they will agree if you can able to give continuous business to them. As I said, trust plays a role here, and it is up to you to make it happen. Okay, now we will move on to the next thing. That question is how to find the best suppliers? That's easy and thanks to the internet because you can have access to their website, reviews, and ratings to select the best one that suits to make a relationship move further. I strongly recommend that you go to trustworthy suppliers. First, analyze the rating and reviews about the suppliers, and start to build the relationship using a win-win approach. Also, don't forget to build trust. I would also recommend choosing the suppliers in the local market if possible.

Fact: 2 – Delivery

Once you decided the supplier, then the next thing is to check how fast they can give the final product or raw materials to you. That's very important because they will also get the raw materials from their suppliers to make the products. So, it is acceptable to know the upstream in the supply chain. If the upstream (supplier's supplier) has any problem, then you will also be delayed in the delivery at the downstream (Your customers). Know from which delivery agents they are going to send the product to you. You also ensure the safety of the products in most cases, that's the duty of the suppliers. Keep in mind! Nobody will wait for a long to get the package. If it is going to be late, then you would lose the customers. The delivery speed is one of the keys to acquire and retain customers.

I think you have identified how to position your business too. You can also position it with the SPEED of the delivery to differentiate it from the competitors in the market. That's why I insisted you to select a partner instead of just suppliers. The safety and speed of the delivery are the two main things to look for after selecting the supplier partners. There is no wrong in knowing about the upstream operations of your suppliers. They also get the materials from someone to make the products to give them to the downstream. But don't ever forget to go with the local suppliers whenever possible. Because they can ship the products in a short span, and you can skip the waiting time a lot more here. Repeat after me! Customer satisfaction is one of the keys to building a strong brand. Just find a way to wow them, and it can be first done by delivering the products fast even before the product quality. It will be a competitive advantage for the business.

****Think it out yourself****

If you are a dropshipper and searching for suppliers in Aliexpress.com, then you know how to look for the reviews and ratings of those suppliers to choose one. Many people start small, so sometimes all they need is fewer supplies from the suppliers. If you are a dropshipper, then you need to see how long it will take to send the package to the customers after the order. The customers should wait 21 days to receive their products. I will tell you now itself it will be the deceiving game. Because the first thing is, nobody will wait for that long, and the second thing is customers can easily buy it directly from Ali Express instead of ordering it from you. Although you are selling the same products, descriptions, and pictures like them. That's the main reason for no sale, and all you are doing is just uploading their products. Why should they buy it from you? Even you are selling the same thing with no differentiation in the product offerings. I will tell you if you do this, then you never make a sale for sure. That was the case for me when I first started my first store with cat products. I did the same by uploading everything from Aliexpress.com using the software. Another mistake is, most entrepreneurs do not know the needs of the customers, and they start broad. I would recommend you to go for a narrow target as much as you can and concentrate on one market when you are starting. It will be easy to understand the needs and problems in that market. I will say it will be better to order your stuff from the local market suppliers. You don't have to wait to get your orders. Another main thing is, you can test the product quality if it is in the local marketplace. And there are even more possibilities that you can go for small orders instead of bulk orders because you can easily convince them by telling them you provide continuous business.

Fact: 3 – Hit two mangoes in a single shot

Congratulations! Now you know how to choose the suppliers, and it is time to test the taste of the mangoes. You haven't got what I am talking about now? That's the product sample. It has two benefits, by the way. First, you can somehow guess the delivery speed. Secondly, you can also check the quality of the products to choose the supplier to move forward in your journey. After choosing the local supplier, it is common to test the quality of their offerings (For free of cost mostly or pay a very little amount if you want them to ship it to you) in the market. Remember, you have not told your requirements to the supplier yet (If you go for international suppliers, then explain your needs and pay 30% of the cost to ship the sample to you). The goal here is to check the delivery speed and quality of their existing products so that you will get an idea about the supplier. Because if they understand their target customers the product will already somehow satisfy your needs of yours in the first place. That's why I insisted you to go for as it is without telling your needs. Roughly, you now would have got an idea about the suppliers based on product quality, offering, and delivery. If you are satisfied, then you move on, and tell your needs to custom made the products for your customers. That is the next step we are going to look at it below. But as of now, you hit two mangoes in the single shot. That's great!

Fact: 4 – Tell your needs

At this stage, you would have roughly got some idea about supplier's offerings. If it is satisfying and perfectly matches your needs, then you know the next step of it. If you want to tweak the product based on your target market, then tell them to custom made it based on your needs. The problem here is, not all suppliers (Especially the smaller one) will do it for you. Many suppliers will also give fake promises to custom make the products based on your needs, but the reality would be different from your requirement. For that, you need to choose the best one with a good reputation, and it applies to small suppliers too. At the end of the day, as I said above, everyone wants to do business, and it's all about choosing the right one. That's what you need to take care of it because I have already told you that this work is a bit of a time-consuming, but worth the gold if done correctly. At last, choosing the correct one will be rewarding at its best throughout your journey. Remember! Business is about hustling in the beginning. You should never give up because the beginning is going to be harder. Hold on tight, and we will see the one last fact.

Fact: 5 – Volume of the product

What is more intimidating for Entrepreneurs other than choosing the product volume? Because I believe this is where the rejection is born. Most suppliers have some volume of orders for delivering the products. There is no wrong in that if you think in their perspective. If you go for international suppliers, they will satisfy your needs based on your requirements. But the problem comes while choosing the volume of the order. As a start-up, I know it would be hard for you to get that much amount of product and load in the warehouse. Especially if you are testing the market, you don't need this much. And that's what you think most of the time and it's a better idea to go for local suppliers. Even some entrepreneurs go for dropshipping because of this. I want to open something to you here because everything has pros and cons. As an entrepreneur, you must solve it and make your business journey to the finish line. Most of the time problem comes in the start-up phase. If you choose local suppliers, they will ask for more money to custom made as per the needs. It will go beyond your budget, and if you go for international and standard suppliers, you must order their prescribed minimum order range. It will also skyrocket your budget, but they will tweak the products as you wish. And the third category is: if you are not willing to spend your money on those two, and prefer the dropshipping, then the quality and delivery will be a concern for sure, and they won't make products to your needs. You need to take a balanced approach here. And try to go for the best option in choosing suppliers that suits your budget and situation. There will always be an exception because you can find it if you hustle more, and spend time searching for the best supplier partners you will get it for sure. Tell them that you give continuous business and treat them as a partner (Building trust is the key). Always think of the long-term scenario in business, and if you don't want to spend time and think long term, then this book is not for you because there is no short-term scheme and overnight success in business. It should be organic and steady. As I said, it will be tedious and time-consuming in beginning, but once you get the customers and revenue, then the budget is not at all a constraint, and you can choose the best suppliers in the market, and it will be a golden egg for your business, but you need to strive hard a bit, in the beginning, to do it and get success.

CHAPTER – 6

"Think like a publisher, not a marketer" –
David Meerman Scott

Begin the marketing with awareness, not with the purchase

Now we have arrived at one of the crucial steps in online business. After setting up an online store, every entrepreneur would think of the next step that is none other than driving traffic to their sites. For that, many people follow different methods, but before going into that, I want you to take care of the prerequisites such as product research, target customers, knowing the market, etc. This book is about, choosing The Right Way. Why do online businesses fail at this rate? It's because they all think about a product and having a mindset of selling it through the ads. It's The Wrong Way.

I believe you take care of all business essentials before jumping into driving the traffic to the site. Does this guarantee you the first sale? Not really! Yes, you read that correctly. But don't worry! There are a series of steps that need to be taken care of to make your ads relevant to the target customers. So, they can take action to visit the online store. Even you did all the prerequisites correctly, this part remains crucial because of the trust factor, and to make it happen, you need to take care of a few things here, and that would be super important to drive traffic for your site.

As I said, success in business is long term, and it will not be worth the short-term players. Getting rich quickly and earning millions doing nothing is not going to work anymore. The process is organic, and it will work in the long term. I also understand people get frustrated if they don't get the desired result. For that passion play a big role here, everyone should be passionate about what they are doing to tackle the slight downfall. If not, there are chances that you easily give up. Now, you will understand better why I told you to select the market niche based on skills and interests.

Psychology of ads

You got the site up and running. I know you will feel great, but before that, let's assume you researched the needs of the target customers through surveys, and interviews and you did some bit of work to understand the market too. Now, what's next? You need to drive the people to take some action, and that's where the next step begins. You placed Facebook ads by yourself and excited to know how it is performing. And you learned that the ads are not doing well as per your expectations. Adding fuel to the fire, you came to know that no one clicked your ad in the first place. It would be disheartening and demotivating for anyone. What do you think? Where does it go wrong? You felt proud of your product listings, and it looked promising, but none of them are interested in visiting the store, and I know it is unfortunate.

Let's cut down and move on to the next one. I want you to think of another scenario where you placed the Facebook ads for five days, and only two people took action and visited your store. But it did not reflect in sales, and the worst case is they just visited your site, and it is not the last stage purchase cancellation. They just saw the home page or product landing page of the website. I know how you feel now. It will kill your confidence because you thought that the store and products are seemed to be promising, but the results were not the ones you are expecting.

What do you think of the above scenarios? I know some of you might have experienced it and felt frustrated. You might have asked for help in some of the Facebook groups and read some articles on Google. Also, you might have watched YouTube videos about "how to make Facebook ad works" and might have tried influencer marketing, Google ads, or any other methods. The worst case is some of you might have seen this pattern repeat for a couple of months without any desired results. And finally, you could have decided to quit and shut down the online store.

All you need to know about the traffic

The traffic is the key to successful ads and it will be one of the most crucial aspects of the ad campaigns because your ads drive traffic to the site. The leads will eventually, turn into conversion, but that is not the case here as we will be looking at it briefly after some time. Some entrepreneurs and amateur marketers usually create the same ads for all types of people. But the truth is different people need different ads to make them take a specific action. Most entrepreneurs are tempted to make money at the very beginning of their business journeys. I know that is important, and the aim of every business on the planet is to make sales and profit. I believe that is one of the reasons for the business's existence, but the business journey is more of a process. Unfortunately, sales and profit may not be in the first chapter for a few businesses. And I also agree that some entrepreneurs will make sales and profit sooner than expected. I have to open the truth, most people hate selling. If not, they might have some negativity around it and that is strongly built in their minds.

I love the sayings of Gene Schwartz that goes like this "if the prospects know about your product and have a strong desire, then your ad copy should start with the details of the products." If the prospects do not know about the product but have a desire, then I think everyone will guess it somewhat correctly, the ad copy should start with the desire. The last one is the important one and most people hang in out here, let's say almost 60% and they don't have a desire and not known about the product but only have a general idea about the problem. If that's the case, then your ad copy should start with the pain points, and ride them to the specific needs. Now, you have some fair idea to understand why your ads are not performing as you think. If you directly go and concentrate on a purchase, no one will click your ads, and this is the scenario of many internet entrepreneurs today. Oh, wait! I know what are you thinking right now. Even if you create different ads for different people still, you don't make a sale. It may sometimes make people to only click your ads. But that will not guarantee the purchase. And most of the time, different ads alone will not be enough to make a click on ads, and even if they click it, that won't convert as a purchase. There are some questions to ask before making any ads and I call it an "ad factors" system that provides great checklists. I strongly agree that if there is a system nothing can go wrong. And most of the time, you can avoid costly mistakes.

Think like a publisher, not a marketer

"When people come to you online, they are not looking for TV commercials. They are looking for information to help them make a decision." –
David Scott Meeran

Always entrepreneurs are tempted with making sales and expect prospects to purchase right after seeing their ads. I must be honest with you here because almost 97% of people won't buy from the website on the first encounter if they see your ads for the first time. Even if you retarget them, only 47% of prospects will react and visit your website approximately, which means 50% of them never going to do anything. I also suggest the entrepreneurs think like publishers here, not like a marketer.

Let's suppose you have a great product, and it is at its best. You feel proud of it and advertise it on Facebook or Instagram. Later you have found that no one clicked your ad or only a few clicked it. I will come back again to the first case sooner. But as of now, you should think that only a few clicked your ads. And no one bought, or only a very few bought it from your online store. When it comes to the ad, there are only two scenarios: 1) No one-clicked it 2) A very few clicked it with no purchase, or some purchased it like one or two in the beginning.

We will see the second scenario first. If only a very few of the target audience has been clicking the ads but they did not purchase. Or only a few purchased the product that means you have not created the awareness of the brand or product instead you are directly jumping into making them buy the product. I hope you got a fair idea now. Do you know why most prospects are not purchasing the product? Some entrepreneurs only concentrate on the outcome and forget the process or steps to reach there. The first and foremost thing is to create awareness of your brand for that you need to create content on social media or any other online platform. With the help of ads, you can make target customers know about your brand. That's The Right Way. The contents should not be created to sell products in the beginning. Instead, it should speak about the pains of the customers. If the prospects feel that they took for granted, they will not show interest.

I also believe that creating value is the purpose of your online content. And, it will not be done by just promoting the products right away at the early stage. Most entrepreneurs create social media contents to directly promoting their products or services. It will not work anymore because of the fierce competition in the market. So, it is a far better idea to provide value through the contents to make awareness about the brand. Later, the awareness will attract the right people and create the interest to like your Facebook page or follow your Instagram profile. And they will subscribe to your You-Tube channel as well if you have one. The awareness will remove the resistance and make people love your brand. When you know that the target customers are aware of the brand and interested in your solution, then it is time to create posts by targeting them to make a final decision. And it will create desire and make them take some action through clicking your website link and purchase it.

The AD Factors

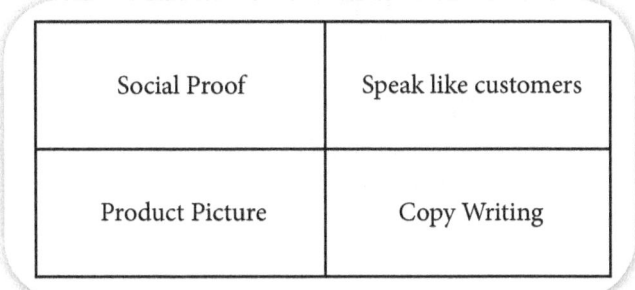

Fig. 2 The AD Factors

When I was starting my first online business, I always worried about the ad performance because it never gave me the desired results. I asked myself what is wrong? Am I targeting the right target audience? There are chances that your adverts were targeting the wrong audiences. If so, work on the segmentation part well (See chapter 3). Suppose you have segmented the target customers well, but still not seeing the results you wish to see, then the following one will be the main reason, and it takes us to the first scenario above. It is none other than no one clicked the ads, and you know that is the problem, but the solution? It is where a system comes in. It will check the four factors and make sure it is in place to ensure the better performance of the ads (They are social proof, speaking the language of the customers, product picture, copywriting). These four factors are the lifeline for your ads. When it comes together on social media. As you might have heard this saying, which goes like "The whole is greater than the sum of its part."

Social Proof

What is the first thing people notice when it comes to ads? It is nothing but social proof if you list the product on Amazon the customers will click the ads, and first see the reviews. Also, note that the ads on Amazon work a little differently because people who visit Amazon or any other established online brands already have strong trust in them. So, it makes them click the ads, and they are mostly warm traffic and have a strong desire already. The social proof creates trust and helps to remove resistance. This method works not only for online business but for Brick & Mortar too. We know word of mouth is the best social proof for Brick & Mortar stores. What is social proof for Facebook or Instagram ads? Any guesses? It's nothing but likes and comments. What do you think people notice first if they want to buy any product or service via social media? It's the number of likes and positive comments after that they may also click and see the page to check the follower's count or posts sometimes. I know some of you may be happy, but that's one drop in the ocean. Because to make this work you have to target the correct ones. For example, people don't like or comment on ads if it is not relevant to them. But the first good impact on the ads starts with likes and comments, and that's the trust builder. It will also give a good impression of the products or services even before clicking the ad in the first place. If the prospects feel good, then they are most likely to end up buying the product. But the case is very different on Facebook and other social media ads. You will get mixed traffic, and mostly you should deal with cold ones frequently. If you don't have that many followers on your page, then they might resist moving to the next step and may ignore the ad sometimes.

Speak like customers

The next step in the ad factor is the heading or the first few lines of the ad. It should speak the pain points or benefits of the target customers. Actually, it should create curiosity to click the ad to go inside. Using their own words in the ads will help tremendously and invoke quick reactions and make them click the ad to check what's inside. You speak the words of the customers, actually their problem statement. It will give you a better click rate on the ads. But don't forget to use different ads for different prospects based on the traffics and tweak your headings to appeal to them. Let's take an example: If someone is struggling to make sales online, and if they have not made a single sale yet. And also they desperately want help to make it happen sooner. Suddenly they are seeing an ad while scrolling the Facebook feeds. Also, it has social proofs that reflect on likes, comments, and followers. And the heading or first few lines talk about what he/she wants to know exactly to make a sale online. What do you think will happen? No surprise! They will click the ad and check it because it will create a great curiosity. If you wonder how you find the exact words to write your heading that appeal to the target customers, then I recommend that you read chapter three once again to understand it very well. Finally, it comes down by identifying where they hang out on social media. What groups are they following? What blogs and posts they read mostly? And, find their interest. You may ask me what if the ad does not perform as you think. If so, then tweak the ad and use different things. Because who knows, maybe the prospects might hang out on Instagram instead of Facebook. They can also read Huffington posts instead of Entrepreneurs. And they can also watch YouTube videos instead of reading blogs. There are more chances that they have different interests over time. I advise you to test the ads to know which one performs very well, and which one is not doing well. If you find a method working, then stick with it. It's up to you to identify it while moving forward and replace it if any parts do not work.

Product Picture

Another notable factor that makes people click the ad is a picture or video of the products you offer. If you are selling a product, then it is more important. Because the people happen to look at it first even before witnessing the social proofs and heading. And you don't need exact product pictures in the ad if you are offering an informational product. It does not require a product picture to display in the ad mostly (like courses). But sometimes it also needs a picture to draw the attention of the target customers. Then the people will look for the information inside by clicking the ad or read the ad body copy itself (we will see that next), and they will also take further action only if it addressed their needs. If they feel that the product you are selling is the same thing and available everywhere in the marketplace, then they don't bother, and their desire will disappear. Because your product is not unique and what's more hurting is even if you spend a lavish amount on marketing, it will not work (See the case study of pets.com). Now, you will have a question popped up in your head. How would they find that the product is not unique by just seeing the picture? That's a very valid question, and the answer is also simple. If you are doing dropshipping, then you drag the pictures from the original seller and post it on your site, which makes it even worse sometimes. Because a few tend to copy the product description also. Are you sure you are the only one selling that product in dropshipping? There are a lot of chances that entrepreneurs who represent the same market niche will also do the same if they are dropshipping. Simply speaking, the uniqueness is already missing, and prospects don't show a desire if they happen to see the same thing over again. Also, some informational products do not require a picture factor here. Let's come to another case if you have a product that has a unique picture. Then don't think they will purchase the product right away which makes the prospects look at another factor, and we will see it below.

Copywriting

In online business, you can see the uniqueness of two things. The first thing is a picture of the product, and the second thing is copywriting. This small piece of information will tell the importance of copywriting in online business. Although, I am fascinated to write an entire book about this topic. If you want to learn more about copywriting and online business in depth enroll in this online course (https://almubeens.com/course). Having said that, copywriting is one of the important skills that every online business people should acquire because it is the salesmanship in print that increase revenue and sales. The ultimate goal of every copy should grab the attention, arouse interest, and make target customers take induced action. It is like touching the product physically or imagining the desired outcome of the product. If it is not the product that helps to give the target customer a feeling, then it is felt only through the picture and copy in online business. If the picture is appealing to the prospects, then quick attention will be given to the description area. If the ad heading already created the curiosity for the prospects. Now the copy, should describe the pain points and give solutions to their problems. It must be an elaborate version and talks about what might keep them from purchasing the product. That's the anxiety part and adds on further to talk about the desired outcome that the prospects get when they use the product or course (if it is an informational product) with a strong guarantee. The most important thing is conveying the value proposition (Self-expressive and Emotional benefits) before telling about the benefits and features of the product. The value proposition is the heart of the copy, and it will make customers relate and experience something regarding the product (See value redefined for more details). Finally, if all these factors create interest and desire, then the target customers go for the purchase.

Do it in your own way

First things First, there is always a natural way to do everything in life. But most people don't give much importance because it takes time. We make ourselves fit in the fast-moving environment and want to do everything in a short time. It applies to everything in life. And I will tell you now itself get rid of the short-term stuff. And always try to play it in the long-term scenario. I love the concepts of ads, and other types of promotions to reach the prospects inorganically, and it deals mostly with all kinds of traffic. Still, content marketing plays a huge role in converting warm traffic. And I strongly recommend entrepreneurs to work parallel on the natural process known as an organic way of promoting the brand to the target customers. But I will tell you here itself because this process is purely organic and it will take time to get the desired results, and I will also guarantee that it will be worth doing and works well in long term favor. So, it is the responsibility of the entrepreneurs to work on SEO, social media contents, and other online content like blogs and other advertising stuff to make its presence on top of Google search for the relevant keywords. Google is the best way to showcase your brand in front of target customers. You also know that all businesses should make their presence in Google to get exposure. There is also an inorganic way to make it on top of the Google search through Google Ad words. The best thing is to go with any one of these platforms below to inorganically promote the brand. It's your choice to choose Facebook or Google.

Strike The Gold

What do you think of email marketing? Do you know it's a gold treasure for any online entrepreneur? Let's assume you have a list of email address with you, and they are the ones who are very much interested in the area in which you offer products or services. They are both hot and warm traffics because some might have awareness of your offerings, and some also might have a strong desire but don't know about your offers in the marketplace. If you have the prospect's email addresses, then that will be considered as a gold treasure. You can easily convert them by sending out a copy explaining the product. Once the email id is collected, you don't have to spend your bucks on marketing much. And the advantage is you can easily create some custom audience on Facebook ads and target the related ones like them on Facebook just by adding all email addresses. It's a sure-shot gold treasure.

I know what are you thinking right now. How do you do that? That question will take us to the funneling concept. Let's take an example here: Consider you have an informational product for the online entrepreneurs, and you wish to target the Shopify, Amazon FBA, and e-commerce profiles on Facebook and related forums on Google as well. What will be the first thing you do? You try to create some awareness about the course and provide some value by offering free e-books about the problems that they are facing right now. You also created a squeeze page or some landing page that captures the name and email address in the exchange of free e-book.

The primary goal is to collect the details of the prospects to move them to buy your course. If they need an eBook that solved some problems like marketing mistakes, then they would need to go further to solve it even more (but this time for a small price). The course which you offer already teaches how to make money online. Now, you have got their details with you if they need the product to solve their problem in marketing. Then for sure, they will also have some problem with making money online too.

If they already have impressed with the free solution which you have provided, then most of them will know you are the one who is going to solve their higher-order issues in online business. And note not everyone will buy the small priced course. Also, some might dislike your free e-book suggested solutions. And, some may like it but could have resisted buying for the price. But you must have to retarget them by offering some discounts to make them take some action. I would like to keep things very simple for you. If you are a math teacher, and you offer a course for the students, then give some free stuff in advance to attract them. If the course has ten chapters, then give three for free of cost to the target customers by providing content on social media or any other platform as you like based on your target customers. If they are impressed with the free content, then they know you are the one who they're going to continue further. If so, make them pay for the remaining stuff, and it's just providing value in advance. You can also target the same customers if you create some other advanced courses in the future. That's why I told email marketing is a gold treasure. By the way, don't forget the ad factor system.

Paying for the possibility of a sale and not for the actual sale

Another thing is worth notable here. Most entrepreneurs pay influencers for the possibility of a sale. But not for the actual sale because it does not guarantee the return on investment. I can see that entrepreneurs are trying to promote their products right away using the influence of the well-known in their niche. But you must understand one thing most people hate promotions in one way or the other.

So do not make the target customers think that you have taken them for granted. Always remember prospects are intelligent. But if you straight away promote it, to them. Then it won't work most of the time because nobody will trust it when they see it for the first time on the micro-influencers page. They usually think like this, anyway the influencer is getting money for promoting it to the audience. It will not convert into sales most of the time. Instead, it is not a bad idea to start with the awareness and always remember you should be following some patterns to make your brand stand out in the mind of the customers. Why are most online businesses struggling to make the first sales? It's because all they concentrate on the outcome that is a purchase. And they forget that there is a way to attain that, and it's a step-by-step process. That's what The Right Way is all about. Follow the same thing when you work with the influencers. Don't think of purchase right away, the first thing is to create awareness about the brand, and it will trigger the interest among the influencer's audience, and that will later turn into desire and action. If you straight away promote the product, hoping that you will make a sale, then I promise you it won't work anymore. You will lose your cash flow, and the audience will think that the influencer has got money to promote it, especially if they are micro-influencers. That will be the mindset if you right away force the target customers to make a purchase. There will be some exceptions, and sometimes you also make a few sales, but it is not the case most of the time.

The thing is slightly different from macro-influencers. The prospects won't think about the money factor which paid to the influencers. The mindset will be like "The influencer is a big celebrity, and trustworthy as well, and they also know that the influencer will get a lot of money to promote it." Why is that? Because the macro-influencers are already getting paid in millions and promoting the products and services won't make a big deal to them. And remember, not all start-ups can go for the macro-influencer right after setting up a business, but it is very much possible in the future. Mostly the entrepreneurs go for micro-influencers to make it. If so, the first thing I can tell you is: "Forget about the sales" and go with the mind-set of creating awareness of your brand. Give away some free information and try to collect the details and use it in email marketing by following the step by step procedure. Because it is like, if they give details in exchange for free content, then you can know they are looking for a solution.

So, they will be very much likely to purchase if they like the solution, or you can send out copy scripts to make them take some action in the coming days. The idea is simple here. Use the influencer's audience to make awareness about the brand. Collect the details and make it more personalized with email marketing. Here I want to tell you something. There is a concept called the rule of 7 in marketing. And it is nothing, but people should see or hear about the advertisement or message at least seven times before they take some action. Now, you know why you are not making it for the very first time. That's why I told you to follow the Right Way here (Awareness -> Interest -> Desire -> Action). And don't forget to make quality products and should be unique as well.

If you want results for the investment you make for the adverts, then affiliate marketing is one of the great choices for the entrepreneurs. Here you will pay for the sales, not just for the possibility of sales. The good thing is it purely depends on the performance, not just on promises. You can use the same approach with the influencers as well and tell them to become a partner with you. If they help you sell the products or services, then you can give them a percentage of commission for the sale. And mostly, it will work with micro-influencers. It is an excellent way to promote the brand, and the pay depends on the performance alone.

Here again, you should have to think long-term. And leverage the power of relevant affiliates to make awareness, interest, desire, and action. You can easily make them review your products, or make them write a blog article about it to make their audiences aware of it. And collect details to promote the stuff through email. Remember, nothing will change overnight, and every effort you make will take its own time better stay in the race to win it. But, always remember, don't look for the outcome in the beginning.

To build an empire, you first need to lay the foundation and after that, raise the pillars on top. And believe me, the final output will be worth it for sure. Keep in mind, the business is also about the process, and there is no shortcut to achieving success. From here, I would like to conclude the outer layer of this book. We will move forward and jump into another side of the coin that is the inner layer of The Right Way. And see how the other contributes to success in business.

THE INNER LAYER

CHAPTER – 7

"Next time you're faced with a choice, do the right thing. It hurts everyone less in the long run." –
Wendelin Van Draanen

What Right Way is all about?

Everything in life, whether it is personal, or professional, choosing The Right Way is a must to get success. The Right Way should act as a guiding force and checklists to keep things moving around in everything you do, whether it is business, health, or relationship. Always try to balance the meter in The Right Way in every activity you do. All the things in life need The Right Way principle to achieve the result. The Wrong Way is tempting and easy to do. That's why most people tend to be in their comfort zone.

There is no secret, everyone knows The Right and Wrong Ways in life. But still, we all sometimes choose to be in The Wrong Way in one area or the other, and no wonder that's the design of human beings. Some might be good in business, but they don't bother about their health and some might not be that good at handling business or teams but they will maintain a great relationship with others. We all will be right in one area and wrong in other areas of life at some stage. That's a natural process and behavior of us. But nothing is impossible if we try because we are responsible for everything in life. Take control and try to be in The Right Way as much as possible. Why do most online businesses fail at this rate? It is because all of them are in The Wrong Way. In business, whether it is online or offline at the end of the day, these are two things (Outer and Inner layers) work as an inside out approach.

Budding entrepreneurs who want to start a business mostly focus on the outer layer, and we call it business pre-requisites. Indeed, it is essential for success, and some people never bother to know about it at all. That is the worst-case scenario, and their failure is registered in the golden number plate. You might feel good because you know the business essentials to start the online business. I am sorry to reveal this to you, even if you have all the skills and knowledge that are considered the outer layer of it. And it is The Half Way. The only good thing is you have crossed half of the journey to mark your success story. It is something like you know all the procedures, exercises, and diet to make your body in good shape, but who would make it out? That's you! And this will land us to another side of the coin.

The inner layer is also vital for entrepreneurs to turn The Half Way into The Right Way. You could ask me about the inner layer of the business that is nothing but you. It is none other than managing yourself well to achieve the desired result because you are an integral part of the business. As I said you know the procedures, exercises, and diet or you have got a trainer to guide you on that part, but still it is you to make it and put your energy, efforts to achieve the desired result.

Key areas of goal setting

The goal setting is one of the important aspects of the inner layer. There are six key areas you need to concentrate on while setting any goals. Those are clarity on your goal, writing your goal, create an obsession with that written stuff to achieve it at any cost, executing, evaluate, and correction.

Firstly, we all know clarity is the question of what and how, but it should be specific as well. The generic description of questions like "what" and "how" will be confusing as well. To get clarity on your goals, ask yourself: What you want to accomplish? How you are going to accomplish? And we already know, setting a goal is easy, but executing the goal is hard. That is where you need the self-control system to be installed to avoid procrastination and instant gratification.

Aren't you clear in the clarity part? Stop there and get clarity on your goals before moving to the next step. Suppose if you want to travel from New York to California (From your place to someone's place), you need to know the destination. You do not have the clarity about how to get there? You will take the wrong route, or you will get stuck in the middle of somewhere while searching for the correct route. It will cause unnecessary delay in reaching your destination or sometimes you will abort the travel program due to confusion and come back where you started. It is the same for your goals. The lack of clarity will not make you reach the destination. So, I would tell you to get clarity on your goals specifically.

After getting clarity on your goal, write your goal somewhere. Brian Tracy the famous American Canadian motivational speaker and self-development author tells "it will increase the chance of achieving the goals by 1,000 percentage." Consider you are setting your yearly income goal. But before going into that, always be realistic in your goal setting. It should be realistic but also challenging. Do not set the goal to earn a million-dollar if you are currently making only 50k a year. Follow this rule [your current annual income] + 20% or 25% increase. It will give you not only a realistic goal but also a challenging one to work on.

Once you have decided the modest amount to earn a year by asking this question "how much I want to earn exactly in the next twelve months?" The next thing is goal splitting. Break your annual goal into monthly, weekly, and daily goals. Suppose if you want to make $100,000 a year, monthly you should earn $8k+, and weekly you should earn $2k, and daily you must earn $200+. Now set clear activity goals, that is to determine the specific activities you must do daily to earn $200+. If you are an internet entrepreneur, you can ask these questions: How many products I must sell to earn $200+ a day? For that, how many leads I have to capture daily through my social media ad campaigns? How many follow up emails I should send to the interested prospects to achieve that level of sales?

Now you are clear with your yearly goal and daily activities. Is it enough to achieve the goal? The answer is big no. You need to develop a desire towards that goal. Your mindset must be "no matter what, I will achieve this goal at any cost." Read that written goal daily before retiring to bed and once you wake up in the morning. Visualize like you are already in possession of that written goal. Yes! Imagine this by closing your eyes that you are already earning $100,000 a year. It will be registered in your subconscious mind because of that mental pictures. It is called role-playing. Keep in mind, our actions, feelings, and behavior are the result of our own images and beliefs.

Here comes the important part, you should execute the activities to hit your daily goals. This is an area where you need the self-control systems installed to avoid procrastination and instant gratification. Evaluate yourself weekly once to realize how and where you can do something better if you did not hit the activities goal of the day. And lastly, you must correct the course, if something is not working. If you are getting the expected results, then carry on! If not, try something different. Repeat the evaluation until you get the correct one. Because you never know which one works and which one is not working until you try. Do not be afraid of making mistakes. Just make mistakes and get some temporary defeat. It will give you feedback to correct the course. It is called the trial & error method. You must not wait until you have proof – You must act as if it is there, and it will come through.

The Right Way of Time Management

Time management is crucial for Entrepreneurs to make the inner layer work efficiently in business. The combination of both inner and outer layers is a must for the successful business it could be offline or online. As an entrepreneur, you need to prioritize and manage your time well to make most of it in a day. All you need to focus on, that day and tasks at that period and make use of it effectively. There is no secret when I first started the online business, I was very poorly managing time. And I didn't know which one work to give priority on the list. And to be frank I didn't have a list most of the time. I casually jumped from tasks to tasks because there was no proper planning of the day's work. I followed the latest trends in promoting the product to the customers if something didn't work as per my wish. But I found a useful technique while I was studying at university. That is the very famous 80/20 principle. It says 20% of the work gives 80% of the result. If you are talking about time management without touching the 80/20 principle, then it is considered as a sin. It is like cash flow to managing time. We all know the importance of cash flow in a business, 80/20 is merely the same in time management. You must have to identify 20% of the next day's work the previous night itself. That's called the "plan it before going into it" approach. And it is merely the mental preparation of the next day in the written format.

I know you think it is easy, but the problem comes in the reality phase exactly once you started doing those works. Because you need to execute the written stuff as it is, and I will tell you many will fail here and give up on the whole idea and go back to the old state again. One thing is clear just writing things down on the paper alone won't work. Executing the written stuff is a challenging one and hard too. Self-Control is the key to making the physical (reality) part start kicking. If you master your actions, feelings, and emotions, you will win easily in everything, and that's possible. If you study successful people in any field, you can see they do what most of us won't. Let's take an example: We all know the greatest Jamaican sprinter Usain Bolt. He completely dominated the sprint competition in 100, 200, and 4 * 100 meters relay races by making a world record in Olympics. Without a doubt, he was the greatest sprinter of all time. Do you think it came because of luck? Absolutely no! It was because of dedication and hard work to the core. Also, it was possible because of the self-control he employed during his stint as an athlete.

There is no brainer the self-control is the key to master time management and everything in life. All people who are considered as the best in their field dominated the self-control part to the best of their ability. Of course, they do have ups and downs while doing it. But the champions will be back on track again. And they will begin to fight back to get success. Here comes the fact, we all know if we allocate the necessary time to something daily, we will get success in anything from weight loss to making a million. But most of us won't do that, and we only write the goals on paper or keep that in our minds (in mental shape) without giving the (physical) structure. People have taught us about self-confident since childhood, but self-control is more important than self-confidence, and a key to achieving success.

According to psychologist Jean Twenge "being confident about ourselves is not the key to success and the idea itself is untrue in many cases." The Florida state university professor Roy Baumeister researched self-control and self-esteem for many years and finally concluded that self-control is a factor in personal success.

Human Beings are weak by design when it comes to self-control. We won't control ourselves for a long time. Self-control itself works as a human, and it must be given the energy to make it back on track. And it will always drain time to time. There are a lot of temptations and choices available to us. We always seek pleasure in doing easy things and follow the free will. If you employ self-control in your life, you can achieve whatever you want. That's why I told we all know The Right and Wrong Ways in life, but we mostly stick with the comfort zone and seek pleasure in doing the easy things. From the above, you know if you want to achieve success, you should have to do what others won't do. And, that is not easy like we talk, that's why the mental state is useless if we don't execute it on the physical state (reality). Stop the talking and start to walk the talk, and that's where the self-control plays a vital role. If you follow your lust, then you will go astray.

Our brain always gives immediate approval to do easy things. It is a great device, but we need to train it to do the hardest part, and that's where the success is hanging out. It reminds me of an example that suits well to relate at this moment. Most of us want to reduce weight, but no one wants to make the diet or exercise.

It will be a great example of a mental and physical state. At the mental state, we desperately want to be fit. The irony is we also know that we need to put in the work, and it does not fall on the lap straight away. We will also do the necessary work for a day or a week. It is because our brains will get recharged with positive energy. And it will be there for a day or two. It is where successful people differ from mediocre and unsuccessful people.

The unsuccessful ones (The Wrong Way) only write it on paper and they won't do anything to make it a reality (physical state), and they will bury it in the mental state itself. The Mediocre one (The Half Way) is slightly better compared to the unsuccessful one (The Wrong Way) because they do it for a day or two with a commitment by making their brain fully charged with the self-control stuff. But moving forward, they fail to check their self-control meter and their brain will lose all the energy and come back to the previous state. If they don't see the desired result, they will fall back again to the same stage.

The successful people (The Right Way) will always aware of their willpower and monitor the changes frequently and recharge it as soon as possible with positive energy. So, they can reach their goals easily without any interruption, and you know that it depends on people to people because people who employed a great balance in willpower will reach goals quicker. Indeed, even some successful people will also get stuck due to various reasons, but they make it back on track after some time.

Therefore, they reach their goals slightly late than the most successful ones. It all depends on how you balance the willpower and execute the physical state effectively. It is the same as a speedometer gauze if you maintain the self-control on high, you will reach your goals quickly, as per the plan, and if not, it will cause a slight delay.

Eat that chocolate forget about the diet

"God created the first man Adam and then created the first woman, Eve. God put Adam and Eve in the Garden of Eden to care and nurture the land. He told Adam and Eve that they could eat from any fruit from the trees except for the tree of good and evil. God warned them that if they ate from the tree, they would die. One day Satan came disguised as a snake and spoke to Eve, convincing her to eat the fruit from the tree of good and evil. Eve told the serpent that God said, they should not eat it, and they would die if they did, but Satan tempted Eve to eat saying that, she would become like God if she did. Eve believed the lie and took a bite of the fruit. She then gave some to Adam for him to eat. Adam and Eve, now knowing that they had sinned immediately felt ashamed and tried to hide from God."

The above story will go that way, but I am very much interested in the lesson it taught to us here. It says seeking immediate gratification is human nature. It is part of our genes. If we look at the above story of the first-ever human creatures, we can easily understand that seeking immediate pleasure is nothing but human, and we are weak. We can see many examples around to support this claim. I would say the best example is none other than us. Most of the time, we will never follow the diet process. And we won't control our unhealthy food habits too. Sometimes we will not show interest in exercise, after a week. We will start it, and we never try to end it. Instead, we will go back to the previous state. That's the difference between the successful and the unsuccessful ones. I don't say successful people never get tempted and I am not saying they won't seek immediate pleasure. But they will come back on track if they experience some dip in their self-control meter because they are self-aware about themselves. They will continuously self-monitor, and try to make their will-power fully charged again if they feel it went low. But the unsuccessful people will try to go on and they will take the tasks at hand with high self-control. But they will be back to the previous state if they drain the full willpower. They never make a way to recharge it again or immediately. I would present it so simple here. The people who delay immediate gratification and procrastination are successful in business or anything that matters (The Right Way). Those who fail in doing so will not be successful (The Wrong Way).

Mission first results second

People we know in our life will fall in The Wrong Way or The Half Way when it comes to self-control. That is why only a few people are very successful in their respective fields. If you study successful people, you will know all they have one thing in common that contribute to their success. They are committed to all areas of life such as business, spirituality, and relationships, etc. They also control their emotions and health. On whole, they commit to their purpose in life. The most important thing is, they have the utmost clarity on their goals. That's remarkable! Successful people always have an eye on the mission, not on the rewards first. It helps them to focus on goals like a laser beam. And, it will give them great rewards, it will make them achieve their goals, and fulfill their purpose.

Let's assume that you want to be a millionaire and that's your financial goal in life. Do you know what's next? You will develop a strategy and also formulate daily activities to be done to achieve that goal. It will make you know yearly, monthly, weekly, and daily goals. I want you to focus on the goals to complete it successfully. If you do that, you will meet your target and be a millionaire or anything you wish. Instead of that, if you focus on the result, then your motivation might be shattered if it is bigger, and your mind will think it is not achievable because it is unrealistic. But if you focus on the daily goals (Mission), then it will take you to the results (Rewards). As I said, self-discipline and self-control play a role in this. And it depends on you to get it done at the specific timeline.

How do you master self-control?

I know what question you have been thinking so far. Being a successful person needs a lot of dedication, persistence, and hard work. Many psychologists refer to self-control as an invisible muscle, and the people who successfully strengthen it will get success. Successful people struggle less in temptation and choices. Even if they slip, they will take the necessary steps to ensure that they strengthen their self-control muscles to get back on track. Also, as I said, successful people never bother about the result at the beginning itself. All they care about the tasks at hand at that time and prioritize the important one (task) as much as possible. If you worry about the destination you want to reach, then there are chances that you might end up weakening the focus of the actual path itself (Goals). That will become the reason for slowing down or divert from the purpose altogether. So, it is fair enough to look at the goals and mission first to achieve your results. I know what are you asking now. How to master self-control (It is the backbone of massive action) to achieve your goals in business? The answer is simple but many will fail to execute it or they will give up in a day or two. That's what will make you different as a successful one, and it is real in every sense they do what others won't do. If you ask anyone, it is not easy at all but possible if you try. Have you ever heard of a story about successful people in any field? They all will make the physical state (reality) work for them. Or I can put it in this way. They know only the mental state will never help them to achieve their goals. How they execute a thing is a secret and self-control is the one they need to learn in every way they can. It is only possible through self-discipline and importantly not to forget that self-awareness is the heart of self-control. You need to be aware of yourself and monitor the changes in you. If you feel a dip in your self-control muscle, you need to take the necessary action to make you back on track. That's what successful people do very well. Even though they fail sometimes, they never give up on them. If so, it is like giving up on the goals and purposes.

A good friend of mine was in the fitness business a few years ago. The entire business was built upon his personal brand. Because he reduced 35 pounds overall to become fit. I saw that he employed great self-control because he understood that he was the brand ambassador of his business. He has been maintaining his looks slim and fit since then. I was curious because I was struggling to control my desires for food. And I never went into the diet for more than a week at that time. It worked like I start the diet and go on for a day or two and came back to the previous state. I could not control my willpower, and all it went on for only two days most of the time. This is where I learned the useful thing called pleasure destroyer. Later, I came to know that not only my friend employed it successfully, but also many people have done it. For example, we can look at two people: one is an all-time greatest innovator Steve Jobs, and another one is the greatest boxer of all time and Olympic champion Muhammad Ali. It is not only them there are many examples available. If you look around, you can get to know it from your family members and friends. For me, if someone has achieved their goals in anything even a small one, they are successful people in my eyes. They would have done something different than many of us. Next time, if you get a chance to meet anyone like that ask for their success story. You will be amazed and you can also take them as an example. Successful people never go on for new trends to achieve their goals most of the time. If anybody has done it, then they will ask them and learn from them.

There is a famous saying which comes to my mind; it goes like this: why to reinvent the wheel? I once had a chance to read some interesting things about Steve Jobs. He gave that speech at a graduation ceremony. I wondered that he employed self-control through pleasure destroyer and set the mind for the day like if today were the last day of my life, would I want to do what I am about to do? No wonder, if anyone had that mindset, then they would be productive as hell. He used to destroy his procrastination and instant gratification by thinking that today will be the last day of his life. I will bet that no one will waste it on some silly unwanted things and useless choices. They will begin to work on their priority tasks to achieve their goals. Another example is none other than our great Muhammad Ali. Once he said in an interview that he used to carry a matchbox in his pocket all the time, but he never smokes. He will take it with him because whenever his heart slips to sin. He will burn the matchstick and heat his palm. And he will tell himself: Ali, you can't tolerate this heat, then how will you bear the unbearable heat of the hell? Sin is a part of desires and temptation and no one is free of sins.

But the best one will repent and come back on track. This world is full of temptation, and we are free to choose our choice. The successful one chooses the hard path for the great rewards, but the unsuccessful one goes for the free choice and is in a bad state without achieving their full potential. All worthy things in life never come easy, you need to put the necessary work to get it, and people will get their shares based on their efforts.

As I said, the physical state is vital to achieving what you want in life. Also, it is impossible to achieve success without developing a habit. The researchers have found that it will take approximately 66 days to build a habit. The Right Way is to work on both the mental and physical states. You have to master self-control by developing the right habits to achieve its purpose and goals in everything. Keep it in mind, people who are good at business activities could fail to control themselves in fitness or emotions in relationships. As we can see, we should fight daily if something goes off the track, then make use of your self-awareness to come back on track again. It is the secret recipe of all successful people. It will make them different from the rest of us.

Consistency is the best habit

Don't focus on going 0 to 100. Focus on going 0 to 10, then 10 to 20, then 20 to 30. And so on and so on until you get to 100. Build sustainable habits through gradual progression – Warren Buffett

Whenever I talk about consistency, I always remember the quotes of Tony Robbins. It says, "It is not what we do once that shapes our lives. It is about what we do consistently." He just caught one of the essences of success. If you think for a while, habit is something that we do consistently. No surprise, successful people establish a routine of something and maintain consistency. And that becomes the root of their path to success. Remember that seeking perfection is not human. And I firmly believe it depends on a person's view on things. The parameter of so-called perfection varies from person to person. If you fail in doing your things for a day or two, that will be perfectly alright in all sense. And it doesn't matter at all. Do you know what matters here? It is the ability to dust off and carry on to execute the same goals the very next day itself. If you look at it, you can realize every one of us misses our daily commitments at one point in time. It is due to some other works that are caused by external factors, and you can't avoid the natural consequences. Consistency requires great self-control. Always make sure you recharge it constantly if you feel a slight downfall because it is all about self-awareness.

The consistency is simply a promise you make on yourself to do certain things daily and develop a habit around it to meet the end goals. If you want success in business, health, fitness, and relationships, then putting efforts continuously and consistently is the key. It is like building a reputation for your brand by delivering the promise you made on yourself. So that people will perceive you in a way you want. And it will not happen if you do it for a week or month. You should do it continuously to achieve the end target. Think of it like you are into the process of building a brand in each area of your life like business, spirituality, relationship with others, health, finance, etc. How do you create a reputation? That's simple, you should do things consistently to make people perceive you in a way you want. Apply the same stuff here too, think of business as one characteristic of your life, spirituality as another one, and fitness as some other characteristics, and of course, you do have different goals for each one.

Let's assume you want to be perceived as a billionaire, and that's one of your goals in life. I believe everyone wants to be a billionaire or at least want financial freedom. But for that, you should have to achieve some goals to make it a reality because becoming a billionaire is not easy without consistent massive action. You need to put in the same amount of massive action, along with a lot of effort, persistence, and hard work. More importantly, you must do things daily, but without developing a habit it is not possible. And that's where consistency will be born. You must take massive actions consistently on your goals to meet your target. The consistency will automatically create a reputation because you have been doing it for quite some time. The consistent action will make you achieve your target and make your mental state reflects into the physical state with the help of massive action. It will conclude if you want to develop a habit of consistency to achieve the goal, then think it as creating a reputation for your brand. And that's The Right Way of doing it. In the next chapter, we will be seeing the speed breakers of consistency. It is about self-control itself elaborately again.

CHAPTER – 8

*"It is not what we do once in a while that shapes
our lives it's what we do consistently" –*
Tony Robbins

Procrastination is the enemy

What is stopping you from being successful? That's
the fundamental question I always ask myself. The
answers I got just banged the nail on my head straight
away most of the time. If you want to know the answer,
then look at the mirror. It was the response I got from
myself. Yeah! It is none but you. Every single activity and
choices are made by you. You are the one scripting your
own success story. You decide on the activity on your free
will. And you are the one who chooses to work or sleep.

Successful people dominate themselves first to dominate other things in life such as business, competitors,
and market, etc. They will decide on their activities

first in each area based on their goals. And they will put themselves into it to become a master. It will make them dominate the business, market, and of course, the competitors. I can tell you for sure if you want to get success, then the first thing is to dominate yourself to the core. To make yourself ready to bang on the target you want to achieve. Ok, but how can we dominate ourselves to achieve success? I know this will be the question scrolling in your head right now, and the answer is also simple but effective. It is "you" again to make it or break it. But to make it happen, you need to avoid certain things you should not be doing if you want to make your success a reality.

Just do it

The budding entrepreneurs should have a mindset of "just do now" because there is no guaranteed tomorrow to anyone. The researchers have found that our brains seek immediate gratifications at present than the ultimate rewards in the future.

Let's take an example here: if you are planned to reduce 10 pounds of weight in two months as a part of your fitness goal. You should start to visualize yourself daily that you are in the future, and you look very fit and classy. But now you need to take steps to achieve that goal you have set for yourself that is the present state. The action is the present state and the result is the future state. You should have to make yourself travel from present to future. And if done successfully you will achieve your goals. If not, then there might be two reasons. You have made no action at all if you're in the same weight, but if you reduced only 5 pounds, then you would have put in some average efforts. That's why it did not make you achieve your actual fitness goal.

If you want to achieve your goals in business, health, or fitness, then you need to put the necessary constant action in that particular time frame. If you take average action, it will give only the mediocre result. And most people are here when it comes to achieving their dreams. I always want to be a millionaire, and I know everybody will, but what gives life to our future state (result)? Everyone knows it already "it is your present activity and constant massive action."

Some people always go on with the future state but never bother to work on the present state. We will be one among them in some areas of life such as business, health, relationship, or wealth. If somebody successfully achieves something in business, then they might have failed in taking care of their health goals. If somebody would have been a fitness-savvy but they might have never achieved their goals in a relationship or other. Everyone will agree with me here: A person taking average action is better than a person taking no action. But still, if you want to be a millionaire, you need to put the right level of action to achieve it in a specific time frame. If not, you will end up getting mediocre results. It is far better than a person taking no action in the present state. But this should not be taken as an excuse to be in mediocrity. Because it will become worse at some point in time.

The Right Way is setting the correct goals to achieve in that specific period, just not too low or too high, always seek to go based on the time frame you set to yourself. The only thing is, the goal should be realistic for that specific time frame. If you love doing exercise and like to hit the gym floor daily, then you can slightly increase the goal to push yourself to see what you are up to in that given set of time. If you're trying anything for the first time, then going small is the best thing you can do, but you must increase the goal volumes or decrease the time frames once you are familiar with it. I should interrupt here. A goal setting is easy, if you want something you make an action plan for those goals. Which one makes it happen? It is your constant action, and that is very important in all senses. The brain starts procrastinating the present actionable state because it loves immediate gratification.

Think yourself: how many of you have started the dieting process but gave up once you saw your mom cooking your favorite dish for the night? That is the immediate gratification because your brain never wants you to go further into the future state. Self-control is a tool that makes you put off what you want now, and push you to go on to achieve the goals.

Think long term to avoid procrastination

Do you remember, I said you to concentrate on the long-term benefits when it comes to business that's The Right Way. It is the same for you too. Forget about the immediate pleasure that is short-term. Always keep your eye on the long-term so that you can achieve any goals in life. If you want to reduce your weight, then think in long term scenario and don't touch anything that breaks your diet because it's short term. If you wish to be a millionaire, then stop spending more on the want category, and try to simplify your lifestyle to achieve that goal. Have you ever heard of this saying? It goes like this: "practice makes a man perfect." I am sure you have already heard it off. It is true because you can change anything by conditioning your mind. You need to practice it, but only practice does not help you in the long run. There are a few things that you need to take along with you. That is "The Core Four" principle to combat the low self-control factor and the short-term immediate pleasure. But before jumping into it, we will be looking into some other side factors called the fear and conditioning to see how it helps you to boost your self-control on high to make you march towards success.

Fear is a great force to create urgency

One thing I can see is that successful people use fear as a tool to achieve their goals. If it does not make you work towards your goals, then it is not worth it. They also see fear as a force to restrain from procrastination. I would always ask myself and others this question why most people achieve a great result in some areas of life, but not in everything? This thought took me to a different perspective and made me realize that they don't have anything to make them fear. They also put in all their focus to work on it, at any cost. This answer just convinced me, and it is very true because most people never bothered to work on their written goals. Sometimes, they do work but not up to the mark. This has happened because they didn't give proper weight to the purpose. The fear should create some sort of urgency to make you work on the goals.

Let's take another example here, assume you want to be a millionaire and want to build a successful business online everyone can guess, you make plans to achieve it. If your goals do not make you fear, it is not worth it. That's why many people set the goals and never bother to work on it to make it a reality. Always try to think of consequences you probably would face. If you don't achieve the goals and if it has no issues, then there are a lot of chances that you might procrastinate, and it will never make your self-control up again.

Let's take one more example here, and the upcoming scenario is purely to explain the fear factor. Imagine you are in your bed asleep, and suddenly you are feeling pain in your chest. Immediately, you rush into the hospital. And later, you came to know that you had a mild heart attack, and the doctor advised you not to eat anything fried and told you to reduce your weight. If not, you will be in danger again. After you got discharged from the hospital, you make a brief fitness goal at home after consulting your dietician. He advised you to reduce 25 pounds of weight, and you have your daily goals to achieve to meet your target and reach the ideal weight. And you see the consequence if you fail to take some action. You might face serious issues, and that makes your purpose stronger, and that fear will become the reason to make you work on the goals.

The fear works as a force here and triggers you to make sure you don't procrastinate because of the consequences you have to face if you fail to do so. The impact will be deadly, and it helps the willpower to be high, and that will make you achieve the goal. The example shows us that fear works as a shield to stop us procrastinate and keep our self-control meter on high. It made clear that if your goal doesn't make you fear, then it is not worth it for sure. Your goals should not make you sleep peacefully if not done for the day, and that's another secret recipe of successful people.

Train the monster inside you

The alarm clock rings at 4 a.m. that will be the most annoying sound for many people because it will make you wake up from a comfortable sleep. Two things can happen here. It will make you sleep by showing the pleasure of sweet dreams and the comfort of sleeping in the bed. Or you will beat the monster inside you. You will tap the alarm clock's head and be ready to experience the pain of waking up in the morning. It all depends on conditioning the mind called "the monster." And again, with the help of constant practice, you can train it successfully. The pleasure is your addiction and pain is your self-control. It is the battle between them. The Right Way is to maintain the meter in pain to avoid instant gratification and procrastination.

Let's walk into an example, assume that you're roaming in the shopping mall. And you see a red handbag which is making you imagine yourself in that, and it looks great. If you go on with your thoughts to take any action, then you will end up opening the gate of pleasure and buy it. If you control your thoughts to wait for it and buy later, then you give access to the pain. It won't happen without conditioning the mind. This is where successful people differ. They condition themselves to pain in all situations to avoid instant gratification and procrastination. If you want to get up early morning, then say to yourself "I will get up early" and make up your mind for it before going to sleep. Delete the earlier thoughts in the brain that will be in the comfort zone for sure. Just condition it by telling yourself that you will wake up early and use your day productively. First, inject whatever thoughts you want inside you to take any action. You can condition your brain to do anything, and kill the pleasure it seeks instantly. If you don't do it for yourself, then take note no one ever will do it for you. Destroy the previous conditioning of sleeping after the alarm. It could be related to comfort or laziness. Erase the previous programming and inject the new thought into the mind by telling yourself "I will wake up early." Or you can also close your eyes and visualize that you're waking up early.

Your thoughts will make you take any action, and make anything a reality. You should have to do what you want to do to achieve your goals in business or anything that matters. Unsuccessful people do things when they feel it is convenient. But the successful one will do it even if they don't feel like doing it. Because they know, doing it while thinking not to do (pain) is what makes them successful in everything.

The core four factors

Environmental	System
Model the Mentors	Youpreneur

Fig. 3 The Core Four Factors

We have seen some of the ingredients to hype the will-power muscle to avoid procrastination. To achieve the target based on these techniques such as just do it now, thinking long term, the fear factors, and the last but not the least is "conditioning the mind." As I said earlier, only this stuff is not enough to combat the low self-control and avoiding procrastination. The core four factors are essential to make the above techniques work well in your favor. It will tackle it well at hard times. Because even if you take care of the above-discussed factors, there are a lot of chances that some things might go wrong, and you flip back to the previous pattern if you do not take care of the core four principles.

The core four factors are a simple thing, but if you leave it without considering, then you might have to pay the price. It will sometimes make you lose success itself. I never take those risks, neither you too. You may ask me what is this core four is all about? Don't worry! That's what we are going to look now.

Four factors need to be taken care of while employing self-control. Even if you take constant massive action immediately, and see the long-term perspective of the goals, always thinking of the consequences if not done, and made your mind before going into it. It's great, but if you look at it these factors are more of a strategy to employ self-control while traveling towards the success journey. I am sure it will strengthen the willpower muscle for sure. But still, there are few things you need to take with you as life support while traveling on a challenging path. Indeed, self-control is not easy to do. It requires a lot of practice to make it a habit.

These strategies are enough to employ self-control. But you must keep an eye on the environment you are inside, the system you make for yourself to follow, the mentors you keep with you to motivate yourself, and the last is the important one, it is none other than you. Yes, you need to be ready to battle against pleasure and choices. To overcome and make up for the goals in business and everything that matters like fitness, health, relationship, etc.

The core four principles act as a checklist to employ the above self-control strategies successfully to meet the result in every area of life. Because the entrepreneurial journey will be void if you fail to employ self-control and forget to strengthen its muscles because that will be one of the main qualities of an entrepreneur and successful people as well. These checklists are a must while developing any habits to power up the willpower. Also, it will be the indicators whenever the willpower drops. It will act as a trigger for you to alert the core four factors in place again. The self-control will dip if any one of these factors may not be aligned well.

Environmental Factor

I directly go into the question straight away to understand how the environment affects the willpower. The wiki definition says Environment is all about surrounding or condition in which the person operates. In an environment when you must wake up at 5 a.m. daily, then you can't sleep anymore at that time. Even if your willpower is low, it will become a habit of working in pain. That's the condition of the place in which you operate. But you can also sleep till 11 a.m. at home unless the environment forces you to wake up early.

When you don't have that environmental restriction, then you start to operate on your free-will and choices. It will be like working in the area of pleasure. The environment has been one of the main factors in self-control, and no one can deny that. It acts more as a supporting factor. Whenever you feel a slight dip in willpower, then the environment is what makes you run towards the goal.

The thing is even if you are doing something daily (habits) in one environment can be broken in another environment if it gives you pleasure. I can say the environment has the power to build one habit and also it will break a habit. It will influence your willpower. The fitness example would be perfect for me to explain this. And I don't think any other because I feel it would be very suitable when discussing self-control in an environmental constraint. That is the only reason I am again and again using it as an example mostly. So that everyone can easily relate to it. There is no doubt! Your environment places a vital role in self-control.

I know a story about a guy who worked very hard to reduce more than 35 pounds of weight in just three months. The thing is he achieved it successfully when he was in an environment where he worked. We were amazed at his dedication, and the result he accomplished in a short time. Indeed, it was nothing but pure hard work and commitment to his purpose. I will always become curious to know the reason behind it when somebody achieved any milestone in life. I wanted to know the recipe of his success story because he was a winner indeed. While examining it, he revealed that he was fully committed to his purpose as I thought, and that made him achieve the result in just three months. Fantastic! Mainly one thing which contributes the most is his environment, which made him carry on the diet process successfully. Also, he went to the gym located on the ground floor of the same apartment where he resides. He had to cross his gym front floor to go anywhere. And he always met his trainer whenever he went downstairs for anything. He also hit the gym twice a day and followed the trainer's instructions as it is. After three months, he was supposed to travel to his home country to visit his family on vacation. That's where the environment played a vital role again, but in a different way. This time, it worked against him. He failed to maintain his fitness in the home environment. Especially! It happens whenever you go home from abroad on vacation.

You should forget about the fitness for a month or two to satisfy your mom or family. Because you might have to attend get together, family events, or even parties at a friend's place. And that will be the environmental shift. Everyone knows it will be difficult to carry on the same strict diet there in your hometown. Because the environment will be very different compared to the previous one in which he used to live. It proves that the environment plays a vital role in controlling self-control. Even it will break a habit if we are not aware. You can easily relate this with many examples in life.

Just imagine this: If you don't have a dedicated place at home you can't do the exercise with the same commitment and feel as compared to going gym. It won't make you get the gym feeling in the home environment. Everyone knows it's hard and impossible for many of us because there are chances that you may go easy on yourself whenever you feel the pain. You would do ten push-ups, instead of fifty because, in the actual environment, you will have a trainer to check and instruct you. But the home environment will be very different and become even worse if you don't have anyone to look after you. Another example is very familiar to me because I always took a lot of work from home while I was working at the office. I will tell you the environment played the role there for me. At the office, I can't sleep when I feel like not working. But the case was very different at home. I can do whatever I want because there was no one authorized to ask me a question if they are not my managers. Relate these examples with the self-control stuff.

Imagine that your mom has prepared your favorite dish, and you are in the home environment, then it has the power to break your diet habits too. It will make you compromise the agreement with yourself and go on to eat it. As you know, your willpower will not be high all the time. When it happens to collide with the environmental factor advantages, then it might work against you. But the sad thing is, you will give up on your goals sometimes. That's human nature because the successful one will give a hard come back again to the actual state. Just try to maintain the environmental factors in your favor most of the time to achieve your goals. Make sure your environment is on your side mostly, in a positive manner by keeping an eye on the ever-changing environmental factors. Self-awareness is the key here.

System Factor

I am very bored using the fitness example again and again here. So we will jump and ride on the other one. Everyone loves to make money, and I know no one will deny it in the first place. Let's suppose one of your purposes in life is to be a millionaire. You can do that by putting consistent action daily to reach that goal. Every one of us knew it already, but many of us would never give life to that thought through executing the task. That's the number one reason, why many people are not rich but only a few. We will see, how to have a system in place to make you go on and do daily activities to meet the goals you have made for yourself in each area of life.

The example of a system is like a rule, and we all obey it to avoid violation penalties. The systems we are following right now has given by certain authorities responsible for it. We are responsible for our lives. And we take control of it by adjusting the steering wheel to reach the destination. Without a proper system in place, we can go astray. We must have a system for us to reach our vision and meet our purpose in life because we are responsible for our success, mediocrity, and failure in all areas of life.

You will realize the hardcore part a system plays in everybody's life day in and out at the end of this. We follow a number of things in our day-to-day life without any comfort. Some of them are non-separable part of our life. It becomes a part of everyone's life knowingly and unknowingly. Does it make you confused? If not, I will be in surprise.

I directly come to the point. Whenever I travel to any city, the first thing I will be delighted to see how people are following the traffic rules. If you see, almost everyone on the road follows the rules set by the authorities. But how is that possible? Because we are still living with some system in place so, it becomes a habit to do it daily subconsciously. We all know that we will be punished by penalties if anyone failed to follow a system set by the authorities.

A system will make everything organized in place. Any people or individuals must follow it for the smooth running of everything. The point is, if you have a system in place, there are only a few chances to go astray. When you are inside that system, then definitely you must follow some rules, policies, terms, and guidelines. Whether it is on the road, office, or for yourself. I put this way everything in this world should function based on a system to act in The Right Way. It could differ for everyone most of the time, but it will be there for sure to make things running smoothly and prevent going in the opposite direction.

I want the business owners and entrepreneurs to have some system in place to avoid procrastination and strengthen the willpower if it touches the ground. Why we will not violate the traffic rules? I guess everyone knows the reason. It is because of the system set by the authorities. The punishment if anything violated. And, of course, the sense of realization that we are monitoring by someone. That's where the environmental factors play its part in the system. Sometimes if we know that we have not been monitoring by anybody, then there is a risk that we may be breaching those things. And that's where the environment and system work hand in hand. Likewise, the entrepreneurs should have to set themselves in some system to keep them in motion. The entire system is in the base of an environment. The entrepreneurs could be based on a principle or a system and they will have one (principle or system) in place to balance the self-control meter. Especially it will not be on the pleasure side.

A system must be some behavior or activities to make you focused or bring back on track whenever you feel procrastinating some tasks or going downside in self-control. A system is also a set of simple questions to help you set the rule for the day to day work. Sit down to write down or talk with your friends and well-wishers to brainstorm the questions which you set for yourself literally as a rule. And it could act as a checklist to have it closer with you all the time. Have a policy, terms, and guidelines for yourself in place. To create your self-system to combat the external and internal factors of an environment and be on it to take care of yourself from any violation. Even you can also have some penalties in place if you happen to go against a system.

There are a few questions I ask myself to set a system in place to take immediate and constant action towards my goals. If it will help you as well, then you can follow these to have a system in place. The first thing I do every day in the morning is to have a system for myself to avoid violations against the goals of that day. It is to tackle procrastination or lack of self-control. Indeed, it is our enemy we are fighting against to get success. A system revolves around mindset, commitment, action, and I try my best to stick with it for an entire day whatsoever it is. I only hold on to short-term (daily) work to achieve long-term success (vision). Ask yourself, what do you want to do today? How do you want to see the end of the day? It will give you a clear picture to set the mindset, commitment, and action for the day to achieve your long-term vision. It could be earning a million or reducing weight, building a relationship, or anything. But everything starts with daily activity to reach there.

As we already know, our thinking will turn into action. So, it will be a good idea to have a change of thought filled with positive energy. In every area of life, like spirituality, business, health, and relationship. As I said, a change in thought will reflect in action. If you lack energy, then you should have to recharge your willpower from time to time. That will be the mood of the day, and the mindset should conquer the priority goals that you set for each area of life. Just commit to the result you want to generate. And make sure it is not a mediocre one. Commitment works in two ways. It helps to commit only to the priority jobs at hand and commit to it at fullest. The last one is the most important that is your action, and make sure you take responsibility for your daily activities.

The action is where you give your thought a picture. It will be consistent action towards the long-term purpose of your life in each area. A system will make us work towards our goals avoiding procrastination and keep the willpower on high. That's one of the core activities of any entrepreneurs.

Model the mentor

Do you want success in business? Then model your mentors! A successful person model the other successful person in their respective fields. It is the success formula people have been using for many years, who strive for success in any field. Why you should reinvent the wheel? It is an opted example for the Entrepreneurs because there is a common myth that revolves around in the world of business, and that says nothing is new in the business fundamentals. It is all about your suppliers, you, and customers, which means there is no need to reinvent the wheel. Of course, you must innovate and add new features to reduce time and energy to help businesses thrive. There is no need to change the structure and principle. This is what I call the fundamentals. It will be the same for every one of us. The disruption can happen in technologies, and without doubt, these are the one which helps the business run efficiently.

Imagine you wish to make a million, and I know you don't ask for an idea from others who are not self-made millionaires because only millionaires or billionaires know how to make a million. The process is also quite easy. You should have to ask for their ideas, action, and mindset they were in when they earned million-dollar and model them as it is. It is a truth written in the golden paper if it worked for them, it will work for you too. There is no sin to add any new things on top of it if you wish, but it will be worth it once you reach that level. It works like a snowball effect, you will get ideas from others and apply it in your own way to get the result and mentor someone who needs it, but this time you will add some of yours and teach others who need it in the process.

When I was searching for mentors years ago, I always look for motivational posts on Instagram and YouTube. All e-commerce gurus taught about making money quickly. I will tell you if anyone taught you to make money on a short-term period, then you should move on. Because I repeat business is all about the long term. I know getting a mentor is not that easy, especially if you are trying for the first time because getting a genuine mentor will be hectic in the beginning. But don't worry! It is possible to get the mentors for free of cost. If they feel that you provide a value for them through your skills or business idea, then they will guide you for sure.

Firstly, they have to feel great value from you or your business. Don't you have that much money to afford a mentor? Then I would recommend you to go for books. You know what? Books are great mentors. So, grab the specific subject books and start to read it to develop the knowledge in that area. In case you are into an online business, then get a book on it. It won't cost you that much for sure, and you can learn from the other person's experience through that book or course (you can also learn more about online business from this course (https://almubeens. com/course)). As I said, if it worked for them, then it will work for you too. But the question is: Are you ready to put in the exact amount of work without procrastinating and instant gratification?

I add my favorite example here: Let suppose if you want to start an online business, there is no secret, you will hire or ask someone to guide you. Mostly you will go to successful internet entrepreneurs to ask for help throughout the process to achieve your goals. It is more like emotional support. And that makes you go the extra mile to take massive action to smash all your goals well. And most importantly, you have to meet that mentor every week at least to get the feedback on the stuff you have done so far. Anyway, you can meet your mentor daily as well if they are ok with it. And believe me! It will reduce procrastination and keep your self-control meter stable. If you are not up to the mark in making sales, you can ask them for suggestions. Because you will get the report every week or month. That's the beauty of the mentor factor! Did you fail to show the result the next time? Then your mentor will lose interest! Especially if you are getting free advice. And there are chances that the mentor might think you are wasting his time and energy.

The whole idea of the mentorship is to make you achieve what the mentors have already achieved. Feedback works like a motivator, but it goes either way, positive as well as negative feedback. Take the positive one as a building block and raise your empire with it. The negative one is the area you need to look into because it is more like a truth-teller of your current situation. Indeed it helps you to work more because it will directly tell you that current action is not enough to reach your goals.

Youpreneur

I think you might have noticed it. So far the whole thing in this chapter and the previous chapter has been circling around "you." Because the real implementation begins from there, it is within yourself. That is what the inner layer is all about. It is to make "you" attain The Right

Way. Have you ever heard of this quote? For the sound to cause, there must be two hands. It Takes Two Hands Clapping to Make a Noise. The inner and outer layers are like two hands here, and the sound is the success in business. To make it clear, you need both inner and outer layers to be successful in business. Even if you have all the essential knowledge in outer layers, it won't help if you are not ready within yourself. It will be a single hand clapping, and it won't produce any noise. You will lose all your energy, waving the hand in the air. When you keenly look inside it, "you" are one of the vital factors in the core four because everything is "you." You can make or break anything.

Keeping up with the monster inside you is the toughest job, and challenging too, but it is worth like gold in the long run and possible by developing a habit of it. All successful people in the world make their inside monsters their pets to achieve success in their field. End of the day, your thought gives birth to the action and action gives birth to the outcome. Even you already know that you should have to make up your thought to achieve your day-to-day activities. Always remember! The short-term activities for a day will help you reach the long-term vision of your life. To achieve the vision, you should work on this day, precisely this moment without any procrastination, of course with high willpower. Decide the priority tasks first and move on with the dominant mindset. As you know, first dominating yourself is vital to get success on that day. If you dominate every day and every moment by doing the priority activities, you will attain your goals and purpose in each area of life.

As we discussed, everyone knows The Right and Wrong ways, but they never show up in implementation. Some will show up, but end up not achieving their full potential. It is the Half Way. Do you know why this factor is inevitable? Because it is "you" who make your vision a reality with your hard work every single day and every moment to get the success. It is "you" who make all the factors and strategies to work to fight the procrastination. It is "you" who come back again even if you fail to control the low willpower to satisfy the instant gratification. I know every day is not going to be a sunny day, there are some rainy days in between on this journey because of seasonal change and shift in a mood. There are some of the situational factors as well, which will work against you. But the successful one is always self-aware about the changing pattern and take the necessary measures to bring it back on track. Eventually, they will take all steps to combat the low willpower by monitoring and recharging every hour with positive energy. You are responsible for everything in life. It's you who make the mediocre to become great. It's you who move from the stuck phase to the start phase. And it's you who see abundance in everything from scarcity. The Right Way is all about complete ownership of your thinking and action.

CHAPTER – 9

"The secret of your success is found in your daily routine" – John C. Maxwell

The Art of Executing

An individual or team must walk the talk to achieve success in everything. It is easy to put things on paper, but the real challenge starts in the executing phase. And I swear this will make a big difference because it gives the result to evaluate a successful, unsuccessful, and mediocre one. Our key focus here is on business, but the executing phase is the inevitable factor in any area of life, whether it's business, fitness, relationship, etc. As I already mentioned, if you want success in anything, then putting consistent effort is the key. Think of how you want to be perceived in each area of life and start to give a picture to that thought through constant massive action. We all know what to do in every area of life, but the real thing starts with how you do it. The executing is the key to success in anything and it should be done with consistent actions. The consistency will make people perceive in a way you wanted in each area of life.

Everyone wants to be a millionaire, but not everyone makes it happen if they don't give life to their thoughts. The sad thing is, it will be a dream and reside forever in their heads for most of the people. The successful one not only thinks about it but also strive to make it happen through constant action until they achieve it. That's the example of an excellent executing! Let's have a reality checking. We always want to make more money, but most of the folks never strive to execute that thought. It is merely becoming a thought rest inside them without getting a shape. Remember! It is not getting a form from mental to a physical state, and it is the reality of many people. We will be in The Half Way or The Wrong Way in some areas of life. Don't worry! As I said, it is a human thing, and it is our nature, but the successful one will always try to balance the meter in The Right Way most of the time possible.

The executing part merely gives life to your goals and purpose, but before that, you must be very clear about the vision to achieve that goal through proper execution. As you might remember this famous saying which goes like "implementation is important than strategies", and you know how true it is? Because it is the bound duty of an entrepreneur to give equal focus to the implementation, the same as goals and strategies. The action plan is where you put the work to execute the goals in each area of life, whether it is business, fitness, or relationships. But without clarity in any of these things will give no results or mediocre one sometimes. The idea of The Right Way is to have great clarity in vision and goals to execute via action plans, but don't forget! The executing is to be continuous, and consistent to make others perceive you in a way you thought in mind. You will give shape to it through executing and open the gate of success that you are looking to achieve in all areas of life.

Mastering the implementation

The main aim of implementation (executing) is to make the process a habit, It will work like a batch process and make you do things daily. After learning the art of executing, doing any tasks will become a routine and form a new habit. As we know, it will take 66 days approximately to develop any new habits along with procrastination and willpower systems installed in place to make any executing process easy. The executing process itself has inner and outer layers, just like mental and physical states. It reminds me of the work of screenplay writers. I could not even think of any suitable example other than this. As we all know, if you have a great story with hooks and structure, still it is like a half job done. What will take you to the finish line? It is your screenplay because the story is a mental state, and that's what we have in our mind or written in the paper. But the screenplay is the implementation that gives life to the story. And we all know it is a physical state visual storytelling on the screen. Even the great stories will never help when you fail to execute it properly. What if the screenplay lags? Every hard work will be in vain. The same goes here too, if you have plans and goals only on paper, it is not worth it until you put it into implementation to take a form (physical). The outcome is the ultimate thing even though you have great business plans and strategies in a written format. It is you who must carry on with the implementation through a series of steps, and it applies to any goals of yours.

Get rid of the emotional attachment

The journey of The Right Way in the inner layer should begin with getting rid of any emotional attachment that is no longer helpful to achieve success. When you're on the journey of success, then the first thing you should do is "get rid of the comfort zone." And you should let go to make a change in whatever you were doing previously. You might have heard this saying: The great things will never come from the comfort zone. Some people will emotionally attach to people, for some, it is memories, possession, etc. Here I would like to talk more about the habits that are no longer useful for us. And mainly it will be a speed breaker for achieving the goals you set for yourself. Mostly, the habit like sleeping, eating, and smoking gives happiness and comfort for some. You need to wake up early morning to start your day. There should not be any sleeping after the sunrise if you want to achieve your goals. For that, you need to go to bed at night as soon as possible, to get enough sleep.

There must be a change in the habits for sure to get what you want. Think about how come you get something if you continue to do the same thing again and again without any change. Do you want to get success in online business? Then get rid of the useless habits and change it as per the goals you wish to achieve. The willpower and procrastination, of course, play an important part in resolving it. The point here is, before moving into the executing phase, you must make sure that you are going with the dominant mindset and use each moment productive towards success. That's why I told you to put domination on yourself first if you want to dominate your day. Whatsoever it is, you must finish the activity for the day at any cost. That's the pure dominant mindset. Every one of us should change the old habits that are no longer productive and useful for the goals you wish to achieve.

Imagine you can't get rid of the weight and achieve your fitness goals if you haven't changed the eating habits. If you want your business to make a million dollars, you should have to achieve your goals of the day to reach your overall goal. It all starts with the change you wish to see for yourself and you should not fail to dominate your day.

Implementation Essential

When it comes to implementation, I could not stop recalling my experience as a software developer. I handled an implementation system in the database called stored procedure. It is nothing but a group of database statements. From there, I have learned a lesson about the art of executing. Don't worry! We are not going to look at the programming language here. You may ask me what the heck is that? It is nothing but a group of statements that executes line after line inside the database. It helps to retrieve a huge volume of data. While doing so, sometimes it can cause a delay. The implementation happens quickly for the smaller ones, but the big pile of data will always cause trouble while executing it. At that time, software developers optimize some statements by troubleshooting it through enabling the actual executing time, and also it helps to find how much time the statements will take to complete it. If any statement takes much time, the concern people will try to optimize it for better performance. They will also tweak the statement, rewrite it again to reduce the implementation time. Finally, they will check how much time it will take again (after optimization) by comparing it with the previous one.

Let's assume you are logging in to Facebook, and it has been taking hell lot of time to load the homepage even though you have your network coverage at its full strength. What do you do? It is obvious you will log out in frustration, and no wonder everybody will do the same. It's the executing problem! It failed to give the information on time. A good programmer will always keep an eye on their program's execution time to get the output. If I must tell the truth, nobody will wait for that long because speed is the need of the day. The point here is, the executing phase happens in order from top to bottom at the stored procedure. What's the essence of any implementation? The same thing should be followed here while executing the written goals (Mental creation). It must be done one by one based on the priority. Once you have a goal ready, the next thing is the screenplay, which is the physical creation. It is the area you plan the goal tactics before executing and analyze the result once done. If it is not the result you wanted, then redo it again until to get what you want.

Here is the example of strategy, executing, and analyze straightaway. Assume that you have created a goal for yourself to reduce 20 pounds, and you also formulated the strategies in place. Based on that, you should do three times jogging a week and maintain the vegetable in the diet with no oil foods. We will see the time frame part in a meanwhile, but as of now, we are just sticking with the executing part. Now it is time to implement the strategies which you developed, and we already knew implementation is vital than strategy. After executing it for a week, you guessed it! It is time to analyze the result to see, where you wanted to go and where you are standing now. Now you have got the result in hands. If it is what you wanted, then carry it on for the next week. If not, then analyze and incorporate the changes in the strategies or execution and implement them for the coming week. That's The Right Way. We have seen only the executing pattern, but keep in mind there are a few things that should be done before going into it. The implementation part is the last thing you do after setting all these things in place. Did you fail to do so? Then your implementation will not be in effect. You know if it is not in effect, then the expected result is just a dream, and it will never become a reality.

Do what you say

What comes to your mind whenever someone says that they are going to do something? People talk about ideas, and some of them are great too. But it is not what you speak, do you know what matters the most? It is, doing what you say. Frankly speaking from the experience, this is where most people fail. Look around! People will always say, Oh man! I want to be a millionaire, I want to be a billionaire, I want to reduce weight, I want to achieve financial freedom before my 30's, I want to marry a beautiful girl/man, I want to get that job, I want to change my company, I want a rise in the salary, I will take this company on top within six months, I will clear all the arrears next semester. The list will go on and on.

When you want to be a millionaire or billionaire, then I will tell you just wanting it to happen is not enough. You can ask me what it is, and many could have known the answer by now, almost every one of us. No, I am not kidding! That's the truth, everybody knows the answer. You must change your desire as your essential, until then it will be merely a dream sitting in the corner of your brain. The difference between desire and essential is a want. When you manage to satisfy your desire from that moment, it will turn into your essential. The want is always about talking, people will speak about many things they wish to achieve, but it won't turn as need. For example, every one of us wants to achieve financial freedom, but the reality is different because only a few people will do what they say. Nothing will sit on our lap without doing anything. We all need to take massive action to achieve our goals, that's the real walk the talk.

Confidence – Wisdom

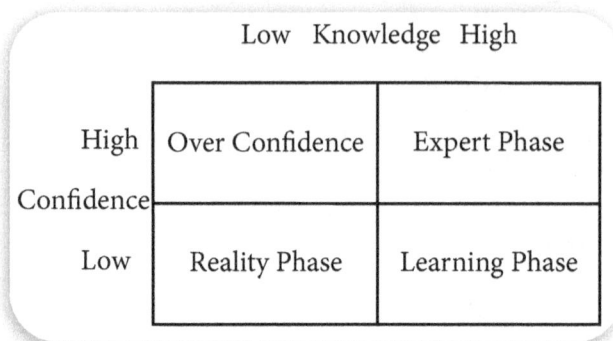

Fig. 4   Confidence – Wisdom

Do you ask me about the will category? People who say "I will do it" are even worse than the people who say "I want to do it." Do you want to know why? This question takes us to the most famous Dunning Kruger effort. In the year 1999, the sociologist Dr. David Dunning and Dr. Justin Kruger researched cognitive bias. It is about people who fail to see their gap in knowledge and overestimates their competencies. There is nothing to feel bad about. We all are bad at certain things, and it is not a thing to be ashamed of. But we usually think the contrary because our mind makes us believe that we are the best in that thing in which we lack skills. Do you know what the irony is? You must have acquired the knowledge first in that subject to find out that you don't know much about it. Many of us feel great about ourselves when it comes to business, even though some of us lack knowledge and experience in the business. But still, due to cognitive bias, we will mostly not measure our abilities correctly unless it is worst. Imagine we measure our abilities correctly if we suppose to swim in the ocean without any lifesavers in place to go to the island. I have found that 9 out of 10 will agree on their incompetence.

Also, people will measure their abilities correctly and accept that they don't know swimming that much. They will also raise their hands and be the first person to ask for help if the consequences are deadly. Why is that? How did they measure it correctly now? It is because of the consequences they might face if they fail to meet as it is. The confidence level sinks into the valley of despair, and it triggers us to ask for guidance and help. We know our strengths and weaknesses. Even though we are confident, but failed to measure abilities, the deadly consequences will make us face reality. Suppose the consequences are not that deadly, then people don't measure their lack of ability in it. We feel confident about ourselves, and that's what I call overconfidence mode which is none other than the height of stupidity. Usually, the person thinks high about their competencies with 100% confidence.

I can tell you, from my own experience. When I started my first online store, I was not ready inwardly. I only knew very few things about the marketing and business administration at that time. I want to be honest with you, it was just the outer layer. I was not that great on that too. The Right Way is all about knowing the inner and outer layers that are two sides of the same coin. I went broke, but I have learned a great lesson. And there is nothing to hide about failures. Instead, you can learn from it. When I first started the business, the confidence level of mine was at a peak, and felt great about my business skills. But the reality was different! That's where my confidence level sank and faced the heat of the actual situation. It was the moment I realized the knowledge gap in my business skills. But I knew this after acquiring the knowledge about online business myself by researching while studying an MBA.

Many of us would have faced this for sure in many areas. In the overconfidence phase, we all will start with

100% confidence while doing anything for the first time. But after facing the reality phase, the confidence level sinks to 0%. But the wisdom about the business will slightly move from "I know nothing" to "I know something." And that's what sank the confidence in a reality phase. People knew that they didn't know anything only after knowing the business slightly. The continuous process of knowing about the business will make us travel to the learning phase. The confidence will rise slightly by 50% because people will make progress through learning it. The continuous efforts in acquiring skills will make us an expert in some area or business. But only after getting the needed skills, which help to move us to the expert phase with an overall 75% confidence. If somebody tells you that they will earn a million in online business or win the Olympics, I will tell you for sure they have to cross all these phases if they are doing it for the first time. Walking the talk is not only about talking but also about doing. In business, knowing the inner and outer layers play a role in your success. Now you can understand why most businesses failed at this rate. They were in the confidence-wisdom phase and did not see their knowledge gap. Business is nothing but a vehicle that requires a skilled driver. The driver is both the outer and inner layers. When it comes to business, knowing your strengths and weaknesses will help you a lot with success.

The story A.K.A mental creation

You know the story and screenplay are mental and physical creations. The screenplay is where you execute the story, which is in mind or paper. To do a screenplay, you need a story. Next, we will look at the mental creation. Because it is very important to make the work on the action plans to execute it. We will directly jump into the example, let suppose you wish to reduce 30 pounds. A good goal starts with a purpose because all of you will agree with me if I say everything in this world has some purpose. You will also have a purpose to make you in shape, earn a million, build a great relationship with a spouse, relation, and community, also to make you spiritually sound. I will tell like this, it is your vision that gives clarity to your goals. And, of course, your goals give clarity to derive the strategies, and with the help of it, you execute your action plans based on it. Everything has a purpose in life. It is our duty as entrepreneurs to find it and do things with it. Whatever actions you take, it will be vague and incomplete, if it does not give you some meaning at the end of the day. The strong reason will help us reach our goals easily because it makes us relate and connect emotionally. It is a bridge that connects the action with the outcome.

Ok, let's come back to our fitness example. You may think why I have been using fitness examples so many times, there is no brainer the fitness example could be very much relatable to all of us after business. And that is the only primary reason for me to use it again and again throughout the inner layer section of this book. To start anything, you must have a purpose for sure. Look around! You can find so many examples to confess it. Likewise, if you want to reduce weight, there will be a reason for it too. Identifying it will be the first step and that will be your vision you want to achieve in the future. Let's assume, you want to be slim. And that is the reason you wish to reduce weight. You know what? That is the vision. As I said, your vision will give clarity to your goals if you want to be slim and make you in shape then how much amount of weight do you want to reduce to reach your vision? Assume, you wish to reduce 30 pounds, and that is your goal. Once you are clear about the goals, then come to the planning part and formulate the activities to hit the goals that you set for yourself. The activities are decided based on your convenience because some prefer the diet procedure, and some prefer exercise to reduce weight. There is not a single way to reach your goals. Whatever it is, sticking with the game plan is the key to success. After setting the plan, you must execute that plan, and that's where the real success lies. The mental creation is on the paper, and it is only the written stuff, but the real thing happens in the reality phase (physical creation) that is where you give a picture to that thought (mental creation).

Identify the Priority work and set the time frame

Before moving into the action, there are two tradeoffs which help the execution of the tasks. Both are very useful and handy for any action plan execution. It is to working on critical activities and setting a specific time frame for each task. Speaking from the experience, these two are helpful tools for any entrepreneurs. Consider the fact, many of us usually think that everything is important and seek perfection in whatever we do. If you are one among them, then I would like to reframe your thought process for a while. I also know that many of you already know this and might be following as your daily routine as well. Let's come to the point, if you think everything is important, then it is like saying nothing is important. I am speaking from my experience here. And many would agree with me as well if I tell that only a few things are critical for the successful execution of any tasks. But the real thing is to identify those activities which drive the results. If I take the sales goal example here, to make $100,000 a year, you need to identify the critical activities which drive the result to your goals. Also, I believe every-one will say achieving your daily target is a critical activity that will give the result you seek monthly or yearly. I also would like to open something here these are my choice of opinion, you may go for other alternatives like achieving monthly or quarterly targets, that is fine and acceptable.

As I said, there is no single way to reach success. The world has a lot of choices and alternatives to pick up. You just have to choose the right one. I should have to agree on one thing here, for a few instances, your choices would have happened based on the situation as well. Sometimes, You could have not being able to go for cycling because of the snowfall, or you might have been affected by some allergy to jump in the pool as well. Once you identified the critical activities of the tasks to reach the goal, the next thing is to set the specific time frame to complete those goals. Remember, you should have a start and end time for every goal. I must tell you now, your task itself should have a time limit to reach the result you want, which we will see next. Imagine if you don't set a time limit to reach your goal or task completion, then there are chances you may lose interest and give up on the overall goal itself because it will not give sense every time. Everything has certain time limits, and doing things within that time frame will be good most of the time. I leave that to your choice. It could be daily, weekly, or monthly goals. Some-times it could be a yearly goal as well, but you must set the benchmark in that goal. Let's suppose, if you have a three-month goal to reduce 10 pounds, then the weekly time frame is very much appropriate here. You should track your weekly progress for your three months goal. Just track each week's progress to attain that goal by set-ting the weekly time frame. If so, then you must reduce around one pound a week that would be the appropriate time frame to act on your tasks to ultimately reach that goal after three months. Every goal must have certain critical activities to identify and a specific time frame to complete it. All you need to focus on those activities and stick with that time limit constraint at any cost to reach your goals. The commitment to the purpose and goals are vital elements here.

Time Blocking

After setting up the time frame for each goal, it is time to block the time itself for the tasks which help us to reach the goals in each area of life (business, fitness, relationship, spirituality, wealth). When a specific time frame for each goal acts as an outer layer, then time blocking for each task will be your inner layer. It's The Right Way! If you set the specific time frame for the goals in every area, now, it is time to smack the tasks which are very crucial for the success of achieving that goal.

Time blocking will be your trump card to accomplish the tasks. Time blocking is a must for all your activities because it plays an important role in the art of executing. Time blocking is about commitment to that particular time which you've blocked to complete tasks. Strictly there must not be any other activities allowed like email surfing, checking the message on the phone, etc. It is complete dominance of the time which you have blocked for accomplishing the tasks of the day. Always keep in mind every moment is vital to reach your goals. If you block the time for the tasks, then dive in and catch the fish. Do you know the importance of dominating yourself to achieve the day's goal? If you don't, then you should have known it by now. Have a dominant mindset before starting your day, the first thing you must do each morning after waking up is to have a clear mindset to smack the task of the day and dominating it completely. It is like you own it and command it! It will respect you and make the time for all the tasks you have planned. You can ask me about time off, all I say here is "plan for the next day activities and write it down in the notepad in the previous day night itself before going to bed." What do I mean by that? You should plan the next day activities in the order of priority the previous night itself. It includes all tasks and time off (must accomplish at least three activities in a day). But don't forget the main thing, it is about blocking the time and commit to it. The day is all yours, and you are responsible for the outcome of it.

Timing is more important than implementation

What is the single biggest reason for start-up success? A few years ago, Bill Gross gave a TED talk about the reason for start-up success caused an intriguing feeling. I had been thinking that idea and implementation were vital to getting success in any business, but he opened a new line of thought into me and made me realize that timing is the most important than implementation. Of course, implementation matters a lot here, and no one can deny that for sure. Is the idea way too early and the world is not ready for it yet? If it is early, then you should have to educate the world. The timing is right, but you are too late already which opened the way for too many competitors in the marketplace, if that is the case, do it as we already discussed in chapter 3 (Perception & Uniqueness of your brand). It is the responsibility of an entrepreneur to make the brand comes 1st in the minds of the customers whenever they think of some category. In that way, your brand will become the first choice for the customers in the marketplace if it comes into the customer's minds. It is about the perception of the brand. If you drill down further, it is about positioning too.

I will tell you now. If the market is already occupied by lots of competitors and they are doing the same thing as you, then it is time for revisiting and you should look for other untouched or fewer competitor categories.

Keep in mind, timing is not about launching the products first in the marketplace. It is all about getting first place in the minds of the customers in some categories. It will be a win-win for you and your business. In chapter-3 you saw the story of pets.com, and their product development error in the marketing perspective, but if you look keenly, it was also the timing issue because those days, the internet was not everyone's game. The timing was wrong for the pets.com, and that is also one of the issues along with other issues. I must agree that implementation stands second and you should give first preference to timing. Because you know, it's all about the right product at the right place at the right time. Now, I would like to go to the implementation because there is a misconception about it all the time. Some of you may agree with me if I say perfectionist does not exist. All you should do is, only implement things right. We all know, the first try is not the one we wish to see after the years. Once we become an expert, the way of implementation will differ and it will not be the same as the very first one. What is the point of doing things? If you do it for the first time, I am pretty sure you will make some mistakes. It is part of the game. What you did was just installing the operating system in place. And you know installation takes time, but later you will enjoy it again and again. It will become a way of life. Implementation is about doing things and it is for doers and action takers only, that's why I said to repeat the activity after evaluating the results, if it is not what you wanted, then correct its way forward. It will make things easy for you because you know perfection does not play a role in the very first attempt in anything.

THE MODEL

CHAPTER – 10

"Knowledge is of no value unless you put it into practice" – Anton Chekhov

Getting Started with The Right Way

I am glad we have reached a peak of The Right Way. Success is all about a doer and not about a dreamer. For that reason, I want to take you with me one last time to explain this book's core subject based on the inner and outer layers, you can come back to this chapter anytime if you have any doubts whenever you applying it. As you know, the outer layer is all about business prerequisites. I call it a business essential, it is very crucial for the success of the business. Many budding entrepreneurs are starting a business online without knowing much of the business essentials due to a single reason. It is because starting biz online is easy and not expensive compared to brick and mortar stores. Have you ever noticed it? Starting a business is very simple these days, like I said, you can do it in an hour, but making a profit is not easy. It also leads to shutting down the stores within three months.

The statistic says it all and it is backed up by the results. If you see 90% of the online stores close the door without any sales. Many factors are contributing to the failure, but it all relates to the lack of knowledge in business essentials and thinking short term when it comes to making money online.

The next important thing to note here is the inner layer. And it is all about yourself, we all know, only the outer layer is never going to help you achieve business success. It is "you" who going to make it happen at any cost, but it is not as easy as we talk. It needs a lot of sacrifice and determination, you should also ready to give up on a few habits. And most importantly, you need to develop some habits in place to fight procrastination and instant gratification to achieve the result in anything. To become successful, we need to know both the outer and inner layers, and it is like two sides of the same coin.

Thinking Invert

Whenever I think about self-evaluation, the quote of Charlie Munger, the business partner of famous investor Warren Buffett comes to my mind. It goes like "All I want to know is where I'm going to die, so I'll never go there." Both Warren Buffet and Charlie Munger have been successful because of their invert thinking in solving a problem. Without having a second thought, Munger and Buffett had skills and knowledge that contributed to their success as well. Especially Munger always suggests thinking and planning for the opposite of what you wish to happen. It will give another dimension to things you do.

The method of thinking the opposite will make you know what not to do to achieve the results. If you want to create a video course, then think of how to make it worst and do the opposite. Why is that? Because if you know the worst way to create a video course, just doing the opposite will make you end up creating a great video course. It is called thinking the opposite. We will usually do forward-thinking to get what we want in business or personal goals. When you do invert thinking, you will know what you don't want to happen. Look around you will come to know, not only Charlie Munger but the famous mathematician Carl Jacobi also believed in invert thinking to solve the problems easier and quicker.

Next time, if you are into the situation to solve a problem, turn it upside down and try to look at it. There is an important takeaway from this method for entrepreneurs who want to make their business a successful one. It is nothing but to look backward and try to ask some questions like what will happen if you fail? What result you do not want to see? If you are looking for successful results, then make a list of how to fail so that you can avoid those and do the opposite to get success.

Model of the Outer Layer

When I first started the online business, I never bothered to choose the business based on my interest. I also never thought of differentiating the brand or product offerings from my competitors. And the blunder was, I chose the business which had more competitors and sold the same thing as them without any difference. The value of my product was zero, and I had a lot of products on my site, and it was available every corner online. I sold the same thing that some established brands already sold in the market. You can guess, the lifetime of my business was thin. That's the reason I decided to write this book to help aspiring entrepreneurs who want to do business online. The more important thing is, I never thought long term, and it was the deadly mistake I have ever made. As I said, there should not be a "get rich quick" mindset while starting a business. If I had stayed longer, I would have known all this by being in the game. And I would have corrected it while running.

As I said, failures are just a lesson because it is good to fail than quit. That was the only thing I regret now, and I wish it could not happen to anyone hereafter. I know you could relate to this if you had first started a business online like me. Almost 90% is the same as this. What do you think about the failure other than this? Below we will see some of the main steps to getting started. But before going into that, I want to make sure that you will do all the necessary steps like market research and some of the so-called business essentials. Just keep in mind, some of the things will be applicable after the first step.

Step:1

The first task for you is to write down your interest and skills to find out your business, but don't forget to narrow it down to a specific thing and never go broader. Let's assume that you want to go for pet products business based on your interest. You know the pet market has many segments, but you should select a specific pet. And further, narrow it down and choose a specific breed and specific product instead of selling all products for that particular pet. Assume that you are a cat person, then instead of selling everything related to cats, focus on specific breeds or specific products. It will reduce your competitors and advertising costs. Don't choose the business that you are not familiar with. I am telling you from my own experience here because you already know that, I am not a cat person, but I sold cat products online. And the worse was, I went broader instead of selling a single product, and you can see cat products at every corner of the internet and even in the brick and mortar stores. It had a hell lot of competition, and even big players were selling the same for lesser prices in the market. And you know customers always believe the established brands, and it made the business survival very thin. I would suggest you select a business in which you are interested and narrow it down further to go with one market niche and product. Ask these questions to serve the target customers better. Are my products based on market need? Does the product satisfy the needs of the target customers and offer value? Are my products the same as my competitors? Will my customers pay me the premium price to buy the product from me? Is it worth asking a premium price? Where do my target audiences gather? Where should I advertise the brand or product? And where do my target customers look for the product?

Step:2

After knowing the business, market niche, target customers, and product, it is time to put the brand in the minds of the target customers in one category before any competitors. Whenever target customers think of that category or product line, your brand must come to their minds first instead of the competitors. Think of the value proposition that you are going to offer to the customers and position your brand on that. As you know, the value proposition is not only about benefits and features always. It is also about emotions. Ask a question: For what the customers are hiring this product? You will get the answer. And that will be the category you should position your brand in the minds of the customers. It is necessary to be first in the mind of the customers in one category. Think of your target customers and write down the value proposition based on the question above. The category should be related to the target customers. So that they can remember your brand whenever they think of that category. Additionally, ask these questions: Are you selling a similar product as the competitors? If not, what is so unique in the product? Are you sure only your brand is there in that category? What value does this product provide? What customer is expecting the product to do? Because it is not about your expectations of the product, rather it is about the expectation of the customers. And finally, what is so unique about this product?

Step:3

I assume that you have got an idea of getting into the minds of the customers in one category, the next thing is the self-assessment, it will be somewhat the same as Charlie Munger's invert thinking, but if you look closely, it is quite different. You can apply the inverted thinking in the things you are good at doing and do the opposite when you try it to execute. But the idea here is, delegate the things that you are bad at doing and only stick with the things you are good at doing. Just write it down on the paper and outsource the part you are bad at or anything that you can't handle alone. I only do things in which I am very good at doing and leave the rest to others. This self-assessment helps me to outsource the ad creation parts to the experts. I work only as a strategist and copywriter here, my duty is to make strategies, plans, and write sales copies. Because most of the time, my job is to identify who are my target customers, where are they located, and leave the rest to the experts to create ads. Always do the things you are good at and leave the rest to the people who can do better than you. If you zoom in and see, you can save a lot of time and it will help to concentrate on your strengths more. Internet entrepreneurs do most of the things themselves, but if you ask me, I will say it is a bad idea. I believe if you do everything, then you will not do anything properly. I must agree that the vision should be yours, but it does not mean you have to do everything alone.

Think Long term

"Adopt the pace of nature: her secret is patience."
– Ralph Waldo Emerson

There is no second thought to me while thinking about patience. Indeed, it brings great rewards because playing long term in everything will give you glad tidings. The short term thinking in business is destructive. I will repeat it once again. There is no short term thinking in business, always think of the long-term scenarios. Short-term thinking should not be an obstacle to overshadow your long-term plans in the business. Even if everything seems to go against you. Always remember the plane takes off against the wind, not with it. Never give much energy to the setbacks because we all will face it for sure in one way or the other. There will come a time you will face difficulties in accomplishing the goals you have set for yourself. But make sure, you should never give importance to that short drizzling. The long-term goals will take you back in place if you do it consistently. I will also agree that sometimes, we all will feel low, and slow down things which we are doing, but we don't have to worry about anything until we keep moving.

When you have clarity in your vision, the short-term obstacles are not at all matter here. I am not going to sugarcoat things by saying that you will achieve everything without any hardships. If you first start your business, maybe even you already have many up and running. You will face difficulties and setbacks for sure. There are many possibilities that you might face setbacks and you might not able to achieve a few goals. But try again, that's where the long-term thinking plays a role. Whenever you face such situations, you should always be patient because there will a season change. The sunny days will follow, after the rainy days. We already know that our brain is programmed to think short term, present situation, and seek ways to come out of it. You may also have some uncertainty while doing anything for the first time. The more frustrating thing is if you don't get the result you seek, just stick with long-term thinking. That is not easy like we talk, but try to remove the short-term setbacks by learning the lesson from it, and make another plan.

Suppose you want to make 10k dollars a month. And, if you felt difficulties or any setbacks, then I would say to try out some other strategies and plans rather than quitting. Tell yourself, whenever you face setbacks and failures learn the lesson and try again you will win. You should be in a mindset to learn from the mistakes and try not to repeat it, instead of blaming the setbacks. When you try things for the first time, there are chances that you fail. And we could see many examples around us, even in our circles like family and friends. But there are success stories as well, if you look inch in, you can see their setbacks when they tried to attain overnight success. I would conclude this part by saying that failures are a normal one. Own the results by learning the lessons to take it forward towards your long-term goal.

Four keys to a successful business

Unique	Value
Personality	Relate

Fig. 5 Four keys to a successful business

What comes to your mind when you think of a successful business? What they do differently than others? Whenever I think about a successful business, I know for sure they have done something different to be on top. Think of an Apple, for instance, it is known for its innovative stuff, also the brand is well known for its different and unique products. Likewise, if you see all the successful brands, they have four things in common. They are unique, and they provide superior value to their target customers, they also have a strong personality, and the last one is the most important one, the target customers can easily relate themselves to the brand.

Unique

Let's jump the other side and analyze why most online businesses fail. From my own experience, I could tell you the first reason for the failure is due to no uniqueness. When the business sells the same products as the competitor's brands online, it will fail. The sad thing is, the customers can get the same product not only online, but also in the brick and mortar stores, then it is not going to make a sale, that will be the truth written on the golden paper. If your brand isn't unique in the minds of the customers, then obviously, the point of survival will be thin. Think about it yourself, why should the customer buy from you? If you are selling the same as your competitors. As we know, customers will always prefer to buy from established brands than the unknown one. Even if you spend more bucks on advertising, it will not help you much due to a lack of uniqueness. Now, you know why most businesses fail without making a single dime.

When it comes to uniqueness, think about a group of people standing together with the same outfits. How could you differentiate yourself from the crowd to stand out? That's right! You might wear a different color outfit, or you can shout out something to grab the attention. Apply the same principle in business, and you will see the difference. Always ask this question, how I stand out in the crowded marketplace? Everybody knows that the marketplace has lots of brands like yours. So, it is vital to stand out to grab the attention of the target customers to make them know you exist. The awareness will make them know your brand unique and not like everybody else. When I talk about uniqueness, most people think of complicated things, but it is a simple thing. Never ever complicate things, and that will cause unnecessary costs to you.

Imagine a guy who first started selling dog products in your city. With constant advertising, he has been created a massive awareness online which gave him not only a first sales online but also started to attract more customers. A few months later there are a few competitors started to sell the same stuff as him for the lower price. Unfortunately, they grabbed some of his customers because a few customers found alternative brands and that too for a lesser price. After a few years, many sellers are started selling the same kind of products as that guy on both online and offline channels that further squeezed the profit. Here comes the main thing, you want to go for selling the dog products online, but you found that the competition is fierce. What will be the first thing you should do? Anyone will tell to you, you have to be position your brand as unique and create awareness about it. It will give the competitive edge and make the competition to settle down by being different than others. The uniqueness should not be told only by you alone, but your customers should also perceive it. If you wish that the customers should perceive your brand as unique, then you must deliver your brand's promise every single time. If you want your brand to be unique in quality, you should give quality products to everyone in the marketplace. Or if you want to be unique in customer service, you must walk the talk consistently. This will help the brand to stand out and make some loyal customers buy from you repeatedly.

Value

The next thing is the value you offer through the brand. Being unique and providing superior value plays hand in hand. In some instances, the competitor's brand and your brand can work in the same category, take for example quality, then you should provide superior value than your competitors. But remember, the uniqueness alone will not help if you see it from a broad perspective. When you see closely, you must choose a USP, and that shouldn't be the same as the competitors, only your brand should offer it to the target customers. It is good to choose an emotional benefit as a value proposition to offer through your brand because it will be hard for any competitors to replicate, but they can easily go for your physical benefits and features.

Sometimes you might have to compete in the same category due to a few options in that market niche. If that is the case, you happen to go with the same category, but you should provide 10 times more value than the competitors in that market. It will differentiate your brand for sure. As I already said, ask this question always to choose your category; for what the customer is hiring it to do? That's going to be the value you offer to the target customers. Whenever customers think of that category, only your brand should come in their minds.

For example, if customers think of quality (category), your brand should come to their minds first. You may ask me, how to select that category? Don't worry! I have already explained it in the first chapter, go through it again. What if you happen to compete in the same category that is already chosen by the other brands? It won't work for you mostly. You can do that if you have no other options to choose the category. It will only happen in some rare instances. And it will not happen most of the time, you will always have options to choose various categories in every market niches in any business. Because whenever customers think of that category, the already established brands in that category will come into their minds. They are already providing the value through that category. It will be hard for you to go with the same category again, which is already there and provide value to stand out, and it won't give any harvest to you. That is the mistake most budding entrepreneurs make while starting a business online. I could also see some misconceptions that most people think. If something has worked in business, they start to do the same without knowing the depth. As I said, many factors are the reason for it to happen in that way, like timing, and being first the mind of the customers in one category, etc. Don't ever start a business by seeing someone else success stories, but start a business online, only if you have a real craving.

Personality

Do you think only uniqueness and value alone help you to be successful in online business? If so, then think again! Two more elements should add to the list to become a successful business. I will start first with the personality. It is very crucial for the success of the online business.

A brand personality is the whole face of the business that customers mostly see whenever they think of your brand. You can build the brand personality around you or someone. But remember that personality should be the face of the whole brand that customers connect. For example, we will see Volvo here. The Volvo brand position is in the safety category. But the job is not going to finish there, the personality of the brand should demonstrate the value to the target customers. The famous branding expert Al Ries once said: "If you want to build a brand, you must focus your efforts on owning a word in the target customer's mind." He also added, "it must be a word nobody else owns." You need to ask two questions while making your brand stand out in some categories. How do you want the customers to perceive your brand? What do customers think of your brand? The connection between the two questions is the personality of the brand. The customers perceive the brand based on the brand personality. It merely acts as the executing part here. If you think of your brand in one word as safety, then you execute it through the personality of the brand. The brand personality connects with people and makes them know what you stand for.

The reputation is created by living true to your words every day with the help of your personality. If I have to tell more precisely, I must quote from Stephen R. covey's book 7 habits of highly effective people. In that, he says to think of a one-word that you want people to describe you after your death. If you want people to perceive you in some way, then you have to do that repeatedly between life and death. It will, for sure, create a reputation and make people think of you in a way you lived, whenever they hear your name. The same goes for business, your brand is your business, and it is the same as a human being. Do you want people to perceive your brand in a way you wish? For that, your brand personality will help to demonstrate the values (what you stand for?) to the customers and make them see it. That is possible only through your brand personality. The entrepreneurs should have to make the values their vision. It will work like this: "Go make it first in the minds of the customers before the competitors" and stay there by demonstrating with the help of your brand personality.

Relate

The one last thing remains inevitable to the success of the business online other than uniqueness, value, and personality is the emotional relation. The target customers relate emotionally to the brand. Speaking from the experience, successful brands should closely connect to the target customers. The customers go through the whole journey and experience by relating themselves emotionally via your brand personality. What do you think of IKEA's success? The brand gives a feel like home if I want to say in simple words, you can relate it to your home whenever you visit IKEA. Also, when you use their products at home, people could identify it as IKEA's product by just seeing it. That's incredible!

For example, if you are watching a comedy video on YouTube, you feel it is phenomenal because you could relate yourself to the content which creates great engagement. It could have given value in the form of stress relief. Next time, whenever you feel stress, you will go and watch their new content first because you relate to it emotionally. That's a success! Take Volvo for example again. People will relate safety to Volvo because safety is what they feel whenever they think of the Volvo brand. Likewise, how do you relate to Apple? Its uniqueness and quality! The beauty is, even before you touch it, you can feel its uniqueness in design and framework.

As an Entrepreneur, it is your responsibility to make your brand relevant to the target customers, and they could connect emotionally to its value to explain the connection. There is no better example than movies. Have you ever watched a movie emotionally connected? It will be like watching you on the screen or could relate to it and engaged throughout the whole movie. Think of business like this and try to connect with the target customers emotionally to be successful like big brands.

The Model of the Inner Layer

A few among the aspiring entrepreneurs who think to start a business online sometimes care only about the outer layers. They are very keen on learning the needed skills and knowledge to start a business online. Like watching videos on YouTube, reading articles, even some enroll online courses at various e-learning platforms (if you want to know more about online business enroll in my course (https://almubeens.com/course)). Some acquire knowledge through reading books like me. Do you think you are all set to start a business? Just wait! If you think you are all set to go, then you are missing the whole point. The inner layer is where you need to work on to crush your online business in The Right Way. You know that you need two hands to make a noise. When you only concentrate on the outer layer and not giving proper attention to the inner one, then it will destroy the business. Note it down, it is "you" who is going to make it happen. I will tell you it is the area you need to take care of even more than the outer layers because the outer layer is expandable and can learn by staying in the process. I didn't mean that you can jump off right away to start a business without having any knowledge about the outer layers.

What I want to say here is, as far as I am concerned, the outer layer is a never-ending process. And no one can claim that they know everything about business in this ever-changing business environment. As far as you are in the business, it will be more of the learning process every single day. I do remember a quote from the famous author Napoleon Hill, which says if you cannot do great things, do small things in a great way. That's The Right Way's essence of success. When it comes to the outer layer, do it in a small way. Acquire basic knowledge and skills that are needed to enter in whatever field you wish, and expand the knowledge by moving forward. Think of yourself as software, you know it needs to be updated on a regular interval. No one can claim that they have the same version since from the beginning. It pops up for updates all the time to stay relevant. As you know, the inner layer is all about "yourself" because you are the one who works on the goals and you are one who puts hard work to achieve the desired results by avoiding procrastination and instant gratification. We will see the model of the inner layer and learn how to set goals by installing procrastination and self-control systems step by step. I insist to write your goals on paper instead of keeping in mind.

Step: 1

Everything starts with the purpose. If you intend to start a diet, you would have a reason behind it. Even if you want to earn a million-dollar, it must have some reason for sure. Here start every goal with this question: for what purpose you want to do it? It will tell you the story because people stick with their goals if they have a strong consequence (it must be your pleasure destroyer) that comes behind it. As I said, make sure that you have a purpose. When your purpose has a lot of weight, you will never go against the goals. Imagine your friend wants to marry soon, but the problem is, he is a fat guy, and it bothers him very much and made him sad. Because appearance may cause rejection. So, he decided to reduce 20 pounds within three months, and that is his end goal. We will see about the end goal next in detail, but did you notice? The purpose turns into a great thing when it is combined with the consequences. If he does not reduce weight, he may have to face rejection that will make him stick with his goal. I want you to follow the same method. When you have a great purpose, you will avoid procrastination and instant gratification. On the whole, you will hang on and hit the target at any cost. Because fear is the greatest recharger and it will make the willpower always stay in high mode. I know what are you thinking right now. I agree that not all-purpose will have the same weight and consequences, if that is the case, you need to employ the self-control to avoid procrastination and instant gratification to achieve that goal using the inner layer principles I taught in the previous chapters.

Step: 2

Have you got a purpose in place? That's fabulous! Now we will see the clarity on the vision. Every goal must have an endpoint because the end is in the future. Some may argue that clarity of vision comes first before the purpose, but I have a different opinion. The strong reason comes first before the vision. It makes you work on your goals. We will go on with the online business example again. If you want to make $50000 a year, you should have some clarity in the goal from top to bottom. This clarity (in the vision) will help you to earn the desired amount. Ask this question, how much I want to earn in one year in my business? It will take us to another question: what I should do now to achieve that? But we will see it below in a while. You know that you want to make 50k dollars a year, then that is what the end you want to reach in a specific time frame. That's the clarity in the VISION.

Step: 3

We just saw the endpoint, the clarity in the vision. Do you know? To reach the end you need to start somewhere that's where you will get the answer to this question: What I should do now to achieve that? That's where the plan comes into place. I believe the beginning is the most important and hardest part of the work. To reach the endpoint you need to have plans in place to take action. The action measures the result. Let's come back to our previous example: if you want to earn 50k dollars a year, then you need to earn $4k+ a month, $1k a week, $100+ a day. Now you know how much you must earn a day. Again come back to the question: What I should do now to achieve that? If you achieve your daily goals, you will reach your weekly, monthly, and finally the yearly goal. So decide what activities you must do in a day to achieve your daily target.

Assume that you're selling cat collars online at the price of $20. You have to sell 8 to 10 per day to achieve your daily target. Now plan the daily activities and stick with it at any cost no matter what. Ask this question to get clarity on the daily activities: What are the activities I should do to achieve my daily target? According to our example, you need to capture 100 leads through online channels and convert at least 10. You can do it with the help of your team or delegate it to the third party to do it for you. Just get the leads from them and send emails with the help of your team or you do it on your own. And the second option is: talk to 100 leads (cat owners) offline via telephone or go and meet them in person, and convert at least 10. Some days you may convert 20, and some days you may not even able to close a single sales. I agree, many times you can't close the sale in the first meeting, but it will happen if you meet them again. All I have to say is, you will definitely reach your goals, don't give up. Think of your plan as a mode of transport. It makes your journey easier. You can reach the endpoint sooner. That's it! We have reached the end of the model of inner layers. Remember these are some of the steps that are essential for achieving success in the business through massive action.

The Right Way Attitude

A mindset is all one needs to achieve success in business. Imagine you are in the steering wheel of your own life. You are not a victim, if you believe in that, then recondition your mind and erase that thought immediately. Carol Dweck in her book *"Mindset: The New Psychology of Success"* talks about the fixed mindset and growth mindset beautifully. And no doubt the latter one is very much needed for the entrepreneurs to get success in business. It does not mean you never face failures and setbacks. And It is not the growth mindset thing at all. The person with a growth mindset will embrace the failure and get the lesson from it and try again and again until they succeeded. They never play a victim role, and it is against the entrepreneurial journey. Taking calculated risk is their cup of tea, and you never see a victim thinking and a success in the same tent. I have personally seen a lot of business owners who are against continuous learning. They think that continuous learning is not necessary. Whatever field you are in, you must be updated to stay on top. In business, you should have to be up to date on the market trends and the ever-changing business environments. If not, you will be thrown out. We all have seen many examples from Nokia to Kodak. What happened to them? Where are they now? They are all great examples of a fixed mindset. Entrepreneurs should have to challenge themselves to go beyond their comfort zones. Because the great things never come from the comfort zone. It will always give mediocre results, sometimes nothing as well. Get rid of the victim's thinking because it will not do justice to you. There are only two choices, be a victim, and complain about life and surroundings. Or embrace a dominating mindset to fight back and forth to achieve whatever you want in life. Because there won't be two swords in a single cover. Either this or that (The Right Way principles + Rich Mindset is an absolute success), and the choice is yours.

Last Words

I hope you now have a crystal clear understanding of The Right Way principles. Business success is only possible if you put it into work. I know many of the entrepreneurs who read a lot of books about self-development and entrepreneurship fail when it comes to implementing because many don't execute what they read. If that's the case, you will miss out on the essence of this book. It will be more of a guide to making you succeed in online business. That is the sole purpose of this book. Always remember, even if you think long-term and have all skills to kick start the business, it is not enough because the action is the only way you can determine the results. Do you want the outer layer of The Right Way to work in your favor? Then you should put it into action. It eventually comes under the inner layer, and it tells the importance of your role in the inner layer of The Right Way. We already know the outer layer will expand and will be seeing about it next. To summarize, The Right Way will work if you know what skills are needed to take the correct action by avoiding procrastination and instant gratification.

Never strive for perfection

"Don't let perfectionism become an excuse for
never getting started" – Marilu Henner

Are you looking for a perfect time to start a business? Or you wish to start it after knowing everything top to bottom about the market, industry, and business skills? If that's the case, I will tell you no one is perfect in anything in this world. If you seek perfection, then you will miss out on a chunk of time while preparing for it. This book is all about knowing the outer and inner layers to get success in business. But the outer layer is about learning a skill or knowledge that you need to get success in business, but I will tell you what, it will not be known fully by anyone, and no one can promise that for sure. The best thing is to go on with the process of learning it step by step. Because it is going to be a never-ending process. If you ask any successful people, they will agree and tell you that there is a lot to learn even in the area in which they succeeded massively. The thing is we can be good at something that does not mean we need to know everything from top to bottom. They learn it day by day and they would have worked long hours to reach where they are today.

I put it this way the outer layer is the never-ending process none will deny it. Some people never get started because they seek perfection in it. When I was a child, I used to learn everything whenever I faced exams. I just wanted to know all the contents in the book, which wasn't impossible, but it only wasted my time and energy. Can you guess the results? It is mediocre and unsuccessful most of the time. Firstly, there is no need to learn everything from page one until the end to get good marks in exams. Secondly, I wasted time learning the unimportant things thinking it was perfection, which was the main reason for the failure. But the thing is, I never learned everything for exams. We live in a society, where we all have been fed with this thought since childhood. It says to learn everything to get full marks in exams. From that moment, we have been thinking about doing everything from top to bottom is the key to get great success. It shows the idea itself is deceiving in all sense. Because you should know what to do to complete it on top, and everything is not necessary to achieve success. If you look closely, only a handful of tasks are enough to get great results. The outer layer isn't going to be complete, and no one can claim that because it will open new things when you finish one. Constant learning is a must if you want to stay on top, and we all know change is inevitable and unchanged all the time. Don't strive for perfection, rather be in a place, take it, and learn the work while staying in the process. Just go for it even if you know that there is a lot to make up. If you wait to know fully, then you are never going to start anything. The successful people jump into the opportunity and earn a fortune out of it, while the unsuccessful one prepares to be perfect in things and they wish to know everything before going into it. It will make them miss that opportunity.

Just do it in The Right Way

The lack of information will cause uncertainty which makes you worry about the results. But I can tell you now, don't worry about the result, in the beginning, go small and think big. If you don't try, you never go further anywhere. I know it is hard to choose while you don't have an idea about it. And that is the mistake most budding entrepreneurs make. Because you are the one who is going to take calculated risks anyway, to know which one falls in your way or which one goes apart from you. And the very most important thing is never to give up even if you fail. There will be some difficulties moving up the ladder, and that is where you should differ and make some firm and bold decisions. Just go on and believe your intuition because you never know what is there, but one thing is for sure if you try again and again, the victory is all yours. I agree there are some factors like time, people, and the situation that may go against you and make you decide faster to get going. If that's the case, just do these two things: Follow your intuition, and gather the knowledge and skills (outer layer). And you already know that you can't learn the outer layer fully. It will expand over time, and you will acquire some knowledge even if you fail because whenever you feel that you have very little knowledge, you will anyway gain some experience in that. Think about it! If you get more knowledge, you will get more experience because you would have already applied it somewhere and tested it.

Just keep this in your mind, don't you give up now, there are chances that you will never get it again. We all would have faced this situation in life for sure. The problem is, you know the starting point: Where are you now? But sometimes you don't aware of the endpoint, which is the most intriguing question: Where you want to be? It leads to uncertainty, but you can beat it with proper planning and with the help of knowledge and experience. Ask this question: What knowledge I must get to reach the endpoint? Did you fail? Then try one more time with the experience you gained while doing because applying the knowledge will get you some experience. Continuous learning, focus, and persistence are the key to The Right Way. Even though you never fully know everything in business, but you can always try something through trial and error which is the fundamental method of problem-solving.

Now I believe you come to know that only products and Facebook ads don't make your online sales. As I mentioned earlier, the business should be taken seriously and you must follow these prerequisites to make it a successful one. Following these steps can gradually increase your sales and develop your brand. The business is all about creating value for the customers (Primary aim), and the brand which provides superior value will always win. And your role as an internet entrepreneur is to make sure that you create ten times more value in the marketplace. Anyway, creating an online store is easy, but making a profit out of it is not. That is why most people quit after starting the business online because they don't treat it with seriousness. I firmly believe that these insights in this book will help you to build a strong brand online. And yes, if you follow these instructions, you can easily earn 10k dollars a month and also you can achieve financial freedom by building a million-dollar brand online. More power to you!